Historic Ornament.

OBIT ANO SALVTIS MILLESIMO P XII RAP IANVARIAS

VGONI OTHONIS III IMPER AFFINI AC
COMITI MARCHIONI ANDEBVRGENSIO
WERVRIABO PRAEFECTO Q DIVO BENVICIO
HOCCOLI ET SEX ALIA COENOBIA CODIDIT
PII HVIVS LOCI MONACHI DESE DEMERITO
SEPVLCHRVM VETVSTATE AT TRITVM
ISTAVRARVT ANO SALVTIS M CCCCLXXXI
H M H N S

MONUMENT TO CONTE UGINO, BY MINO DA FIESOLE,
CHURCH OF THE BADIA, FLORENCE.

A Manual of
HISTORIC
ORNAMENT

TREATING UPON THE EVOLUTION, TRADITION, AND DEVELOPMENT OF ARCHITECTURE & THE APPLIED ARTS

PREPARED FOR THE USE OF STUDENTS AND CRAFTSMEN

BY RICHARD GLAZIER

HON. ASSOCIATE OF THE ROYAL COLLEGE OF ART
ASSOCIATE OF THE ROYAL INSTITUTE OF BRITISH ARCHITECTS
HEAD MASTER OF THE MUNICIPAL SCHOOL OF ART, MANCHESTER

SECOND EDITION, REVISED AND ENLARGED
WITH 600 ILLUSTRATIONS BY THE AUTHOR

· · ·

LONDON
B. T. BATSFORD, 94 HIGH HOLBORN
MCMVI

INTRO TO THE ABACUS EDITION

In an age dominated by mass production and digital replication, the tactile wisdom embedded in our architectural heritage stands quietly resilient. Richard Glazier's *A Manual of Historic Ornament* reemerges from historical obscurity not merely as documentation but as an essential bridge reconnecting contemporary architectural literacy with the nuanced craftsmanship of the past.

Richard Glazier (1851–1918) occupies a pivotal position in late Victorian art and architectural education. Though formally trained as an architect—he became an Associate of the Royal Institute of British Architects in 1892—Glazier chose to dedicate himself fully to teaching, rather than private practice. His 26-year tenure as headmaster at Manchester Municipal School of Art placed him at the heart of one of Britain's most innovative institutions during a period marked by rapid industrial and cultural change.

Glazier's career navigated two significant currents shaping Victorian design philosophy. Industrialization had brought about unprecedented production capacity, crafting ornaments with mechanical precision yet often sacrificing the subtlety and artistry intrinsic to hand craftsmanship. Concurrently, figures like William Morris and John Ruskin passionately advocated for a return to pre-industrial principles, emphasizing the intimate relationship between designers and their materials. Glazier stood precisely at this intersection, embodying the tension between industrial efficiency and handcrafted tradition, profoundly influencing his educational methodology.

First published in 1899, with a notably expanded second edition in 1907, Glazier's manual addressed urgent concerns of his time—that mass production was severing the connection between ornamentation and the practical mastery of materials. As Glazier himself explained, his intent was to guide students and craftsmen toward appreciating "the beauty, suggestiveness, and vitality of the Industrial arts of the past, and their intimate relation to the social and religious life of the people."

Unlike contemporary pattern books designed merely for replication, Glazier's work offers an evolutionary exploration of ornament, tracing design principles across diverse cultures and materials rather than promoting superficial copying. With over 600 illustrations ranging from ancient Egyptian motifs to Renaissance furniture and intricate Gothic details, the manual serves as a comprehensive survey of ornamental history. The expanded second edition notably enhances architectural coverage, adding crucial insights into Greek, Romanesque, Gothic, and Renaissance styles.

Today, as we experience a resurgence of interest in authentic craftsmanship and the expressive potential of materials, Glazier's manual has acquired renewed significance. The expertise captured in its pages was nearly eclipsed during modernism's rejection of ornamentation throughout the early 20th century. When Adolf Loos famously declared "ornament is crime" in 1908, it presaged a century of architectural education increasingly divorced from decorative traditions.

This knowledge gap continues to pose practical challenges for modern architects and preservationists tasked with restoring historic structures. Glazier's manual provides invaluable clarity into the evolution of ornamental techniques, materials, tools, and cultural context. Each meticulously illustrated example conveys not just aesthetic value but embodies generations of accumulated craft intelligence.

For contemporary readers, Glazier's manual offers rich and varied perspectives. Preservation architects will find precise documentation of ornamental details largely omitted from modern curricula. Designers searching for sustainable, localized production methods will gain insights into historic practices. Craftspeople participating in today's revival of artisanal economies will discover ornamentation as an organic expression of material qualities, rather than superficial decoration.

Beyond practical applications, the manual advocates for a deeper understanding of historical continuity and cultural context as fundamental to meaningful design. Glazier demonstrates that architectural ornamentation historically served as a sophisticated visual language, connecting structures to their societal roles and temporal context.

At Abacus Press, we recognize architectural wisdom as a cumulative legacy, easily endangered by neglect. Our mission to resurrect overlooked architectural knowledge is perfectly embodied in Glazier's seminal work. By returning *A Manual of Historic Ornament* to modern circulation, we reaffirm our dedication to enriching contemporary architectural practice through historical insight.

We present this edition not merely as a historical curiosity, but as an active resource for architects, designers, preservationists, and craftspeople striving to integrate tradition with innovation. As Glazier himself expressed, the benefits of studying historic ornamentation include understanding "the capabilities and limitations of material, the appropriateness and application of ornament," and "the interest and significance of detail."

May this reprinted edition serve both as an homage to past mastery and a catalyst for future creativity.

PREFACE TO THE SECOND EDITION.

THE extreme range of subjects included under Historic Ornament necessarily implies considerable restriction and condensation in text and illustration in one small volume, yet care has been taken in the selection of types to show the essentials and characteristics of national styles, and the evolution or development of design in various materials.

The re-issue of this work has enabled the author to revise generally and also to add additional matter and illustrations in the more important sections.

The subject of Architecture has received considerable amplification, as additional illustrations are given of the Greek, Romanesque, and Gothic styles, together with the Italian, French, and English Renascence, making this branch of the work more comprehensive and useful to the general reader.

The section dealing with the applied arts has also been enlarged, additional plates of Gold and Silver, Bronzes, Furniture, Woodcarvings, and Bookbindings being inserted, together with a number of the beautiful initial letters of the early printed books of the latter part of the 15th and the early 16th centuries, illustrating the vitality, inventiveness, and skill of the craftsmen of the past.

R. G.

MANCHESTER,
1906.

PREFACE.

This manual has been prepared with the three-fold object of giving an elementary knowledge of Architecture and Historic Ornament, of awakening a responsive and sympathetic feeling for the many beautiful and interesting remains of ancient and mediæval civilization, and lastly, of directing the attention of students and craftsmen to the beauty, suggestiveness, and vitality of the Industrial arts of the past, and their intimate relation to the social and religious life of the people.

The advantages to be derived by students and craftsmen from such a study are manifold, for, by a careful study of these arts we may see the capabilities and limitations of material, the appropriateness and application of ornament, the continuity of line and form—yet with a marked diversity of enrichment and treatment—the interest and significance of detail, and the customs, myths, and traditions of the past, with their continuity of thought and expression.

The illustrations, which have been chosen expressly for this work, are typical examples of each period or style and are produced in line as being the method best suited to the requirements of students, giving definition, emphasis, and constructive qualities of design rather than pictorial effect.

In the appendix will be found a list of text-books and works of reference, which may be studied with considerable advantage by students desiring further information upon this important subject.

RICHARD GLAZIER.

MANCHESTER,
1899.

CONTENTS.

LIST OF PLATES.

ILLUSTRATIONS IN THE TEXT.

CORRECTIONS.

Page 23, *line* 11, *for* " Maxentinus " *read* " Maxentius."
,, 23, ,, 29, ,, " Conpluvium " *read* " Compluvium."
,, 25, *illustration* " Temple of Peace " *read* " Basilica of Maxentius."
,, 27, *line* 31, *for* " tazzas " *read* " tazze."
,, 29, ,, 20, ,, " plate 33 " *read* " plate 34."
,, 31, ,, 35, ,, " plate 53 " *read* " plate 54."
,, 35, ,, 29, ,, " page 116 " *read* " page 117."
,, 40, ,, 28, ,, " plate 18 " *read* " plate 15."
,, 53, ,, 38, ,, " page 153 " *read* " page 155."
,, 55, ,, 38, ,, " S. Eustovgio " *read* " S. Eustorgio."
,, 57, ,, 3, ,, " plate 43 " *read* " plate 44."
,, 62, ,, 45, ,, " plate 19 " *read* " plate 22."
,, 69, ,, 43, ,, " plate 35 " *read* " plate 36."
,, 69, ,, 44, ,, " plate 47 " *read* " plate 48."
,, 69, ,, 42. ,, " Andronet " *read* " Androuet."
,, 71, ,, 6, ,, " De Carreau and Duperie " *read* " Du Cerceau and Duperac."
,, 71, *lines* 12 *and* 28, *for* " plates 47-50 " *read* " plates 48-51."
,, 77, *line* 14, *for* " Radcliffe Library " *read* " Radcliffe Library, Oxford."
,, 77, ,, 27, ,, " Pergolese " *read* " Pergolesi."
,, 103, ,, 3, ,, " plate 34 " *read* " plate 35."
,, 129, ,, 43, ,, " page 44 " *read* " page 56."
,, 131, ,, 20, ,, " plate 46 " *read* " plate 47."
,, 151, ,, 17, ,, " Suetonius of 1740 " *read* " 1470."
,, 153, ,, 34, ,, " pages 101 and 147 " *read* " pages 103 and 149."

Part I.
The History and Development of Architecture & Ornament.

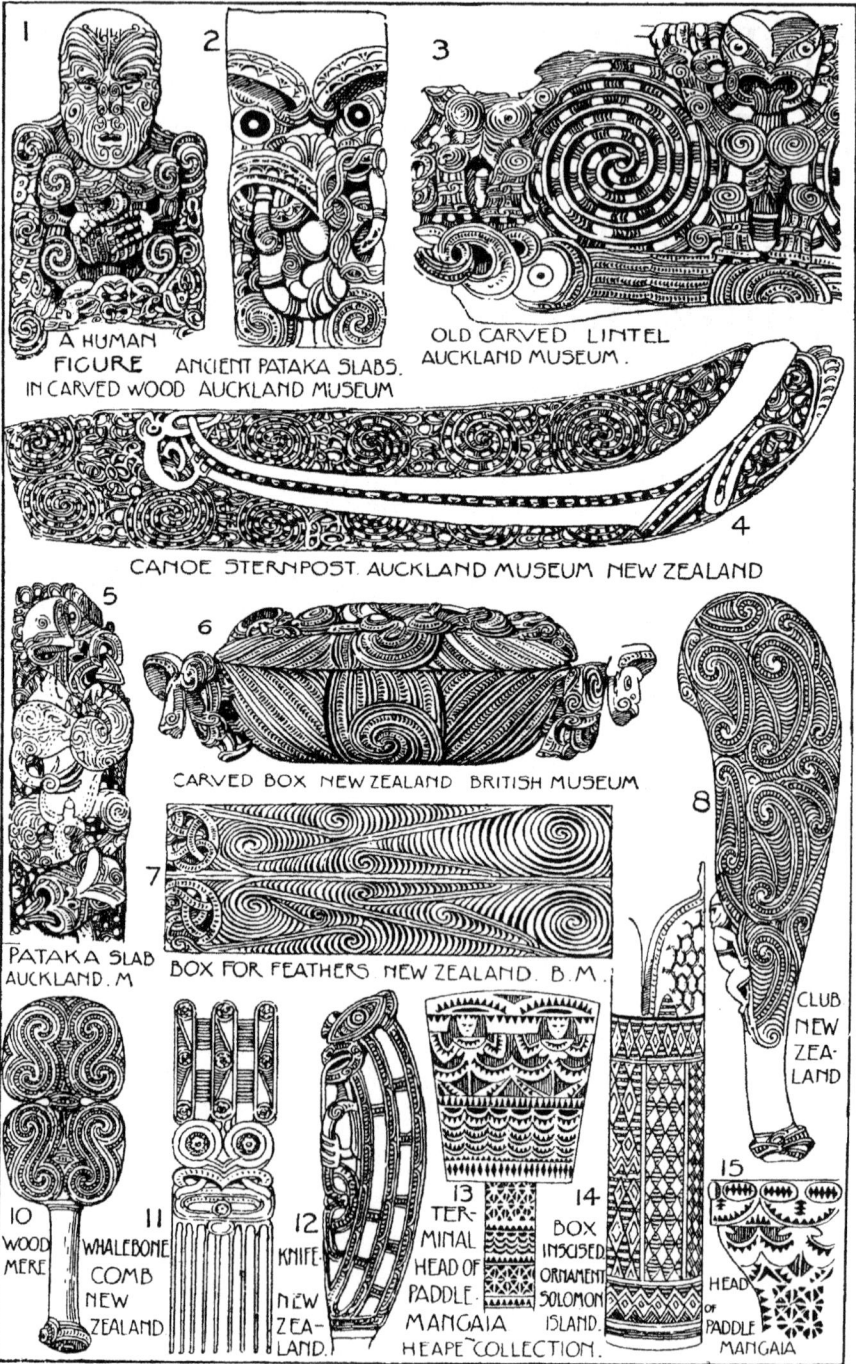

1 A HUMAN FIGURE IN CARVED WOOD AUCKLAND MUSEUM

2 ANCIENT PATAKA SLABS.

3 OLD CARVED LINTEL AUCKLAND MUSEUM.

4 CANOE STERNPOST. AUCKLAND MUSEUM NEW ZEALAND

5 PATAKA SLAB AUCKLAND. M

6 CARVED BOX NEW ZEALAND BRITISH MUSEUM

7 BOX FOR FEATHERS NEW ZEALAND. B.M.

8 CLUB NEW ZEALAND

10 WOOD MERE

11 WHALEBONE COMB NEW ZEALAND

12 KNIFE NEW ZEALAND.

13 TERMINAL HEAD OF PADDLE MANGAIA

14 BOX INCISED ORNAMENT SOLOMON ISLAND.

15 HEAD OF PADDLE MANGAIA

HEAPE COLLECTION.

ORNAMENT OF OCEANIA.

The ornamentation of the people of the Pacific Isles is full of interest, and is remarkable for the evolution and perfecting of an ornamental style by a primitive people, with myths and traditions purely local, and in no way influenced by other nations. It is a style of ornament full of meaning and symbolism, yet simple in detail and arrangement, not founded upon the beautiful vegetation and flora of their islands, but upon abstract forms derived from the human figure, and arranged with a pleasing geometrical precision remarkable for a primitive people.

The ornamental art of these people may be broadly divided into provinces, each with its distinct ornamental characteristics and traditions, New Zealand showing the highest development and Australia the lowest in the ornament of Polynesia and Melanesia.

Much of the ornament is purely linear, consisting of parallel and zig-zag lines; that of Australia consists almost entirely of these lines incised in the ground and occasionally filled in with colour. In New Guinea a higher development is reached, the ornament, of straight and curved lines, being carved in flat relief. In the province of Tonga-Samoa, the surface is divided into small fields, and the linear ornament runs in a different direction on each of the fields. The Hervey and Austral Islands are distinguished by their remarkable adaptations of the human female figure, the illustrations given here showing the original type and its ornamental development. These examples, together with the circular eye pattern, form the elements of the Hervey province, of which the Heape collection contains many

fine examples. In the Solomon Island the linear ornament is occasionally interspersed with an inlay of angular pieces of mother of pearl. The New Zealand province is distinguished by its skilful pierced carving, the beauty of its spiral forms adapted from the human figure (figs. 1-12), and the constant use of the border here given.

3

WINGED GLOBE AND ASPS.

2

THE SCARABŒUS OR SACRED BEETLE.

HATHORIC CAPITAL SUR-
MOUNTED BY A NAOS · PHILÆ·
B.C. 106

3

4　5

COLUMNS FROM THEBES B.C. 1250.

6

RELIEF FROM THE BRITISH MUSEUM.

16

15

THE EGYPTIAN LOTUS.

7

8

9

10

EXAMPLES OF PAINTED ORNAMENT. 1800 B.C.

EGYPTIAN ORNAMENT.

The history of Egypt, extending from 4400 B.C. to 340 B.C., during which thirty dynasties existed, is usually divided into three groups: (1) The Ancient Empire, I.-XI. dynasties, 4400-2466 B.C.; (2) The Middle Empire, XII.-XIX., 2466-1200 B.C.; and (3) the New Empire, XX.-XXX. dynasties, 1200-340 B.C.

The capitals of the Ancient Empire comprised Memphis and Abydos; of the Middle Empire, Thebes, Luxor, and Tanis; and of the New Empire, Sais and Bubastes. The remarkable civilization of these early dynasties is attested by the many fine remains of architecture, sculpture, and decorative arts that enrich our national museums. The Great Pyramids were built during the 4th dynasty, the largest by Kheops, 3733-3700 B.C., is 756 ft. by 756 ft., and 480 ft. high; the second, by Kephren, 3666-3633 B.C., is 707 ft. by 707 ft. and 454 ft. high; and the third, 333 ft. by 330 ft., and 218 ft. high, was erected by Mykerinos, 3633-3600 B.C.

The Sphinx, half animal and half human, is the oldest sculpture known, and is probably of the 1st and 2nd dynasties, yet it is singular that all the earliest sculptures of the 3rd and 4th dynasties with which we are acquainted were realistic portraiture, remarkable for fidelity to nature. Kings, queens, and individuals of note were finely sculptured, frequently of a colossal size. But the Deities, Amen Sckhet, Horus, Hathor, Iris, and Osiris were represented in the later dynasties by small votive statuettes, noticeable for their number rather than for their artistic qualities, never reaching the excellence or vitality of the earlier period. Much of the architectural enrichment was in *Cavo Relievo*, a peculiarly Egyptian mode of ornamentation, the outline of the figures, birds, or flowers being sunk into the surface of the granite or basalt, and then carved within this sunk outline, leaving the ground or bed raised, these reliefs being invariably painted red, blue, green, and yellow. The frieze which in the hands of the Greeks, at a later period, became their principal ornamental field, was used by the Egyptians in superposed bands, showing, in *cavo relievo*, the industrial arts and pursuits—weaving, glass blowing, and the making of pottery; ploughing, sowing, and reaping; also hunting and fishing. The composition and sculpture of these incidents was simple, refined, and purely decorative, with a *naïveté* and unaffectedness so appropriate to the architectonic conditions. Mingled with these incidents were the beautiful hieroglyphs, or picture writing of the Egyptians. Figs. 7-13 are examples of painted decorations showing the spiral construction of lines, together with the symbolic treatment of the Lotus, the latter being regarded by the Egyptians as a symbol of fertility and of a new life, hence the profusion with which it was used in their decorative work. Great fertility of invention was displayed in enriching their architectural capitals with the Lotus, the Papyrus, and the Palm. A singular feature introduced during the 18th dynasty was the Hathor Capital, surmounted by a small Naos. During the Ptolemaic period— B.C. 300—the Hathor Capital was placed upon the vertical bell-shaped capital (fig. 3).

5

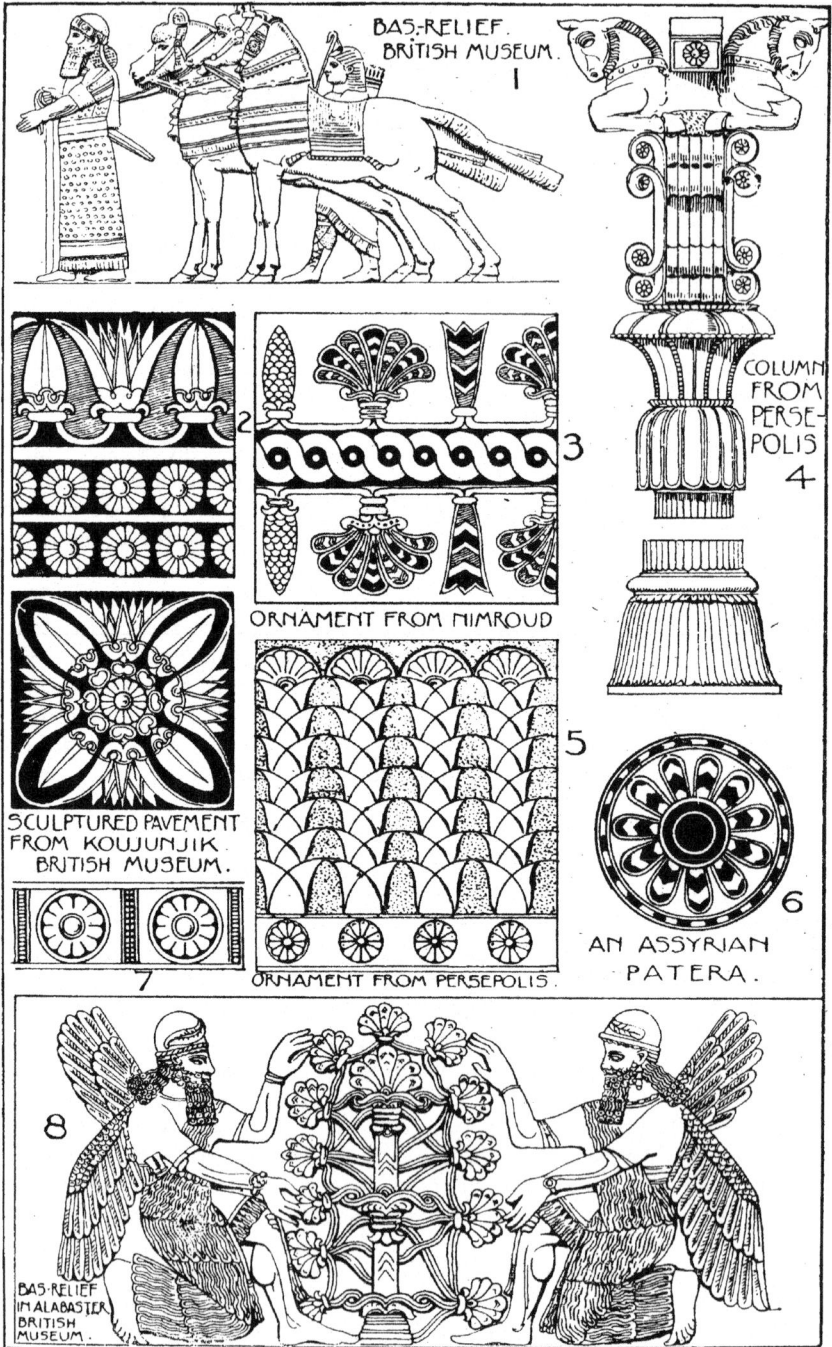

BAS-RELIEF.
BRITISH MUSEUM.
1

COLUMN
FROM
PERSE-
POLIS
4

2

3

ORNAMENT FROM NIMROUD

5

SCULPTURED PAVEMENT
FROM KOUJUNJIK.
BRITISH MUSEUM.

6

AN ASSYRIAN
PATERA.

7

ORNAMENT FROM PERSEPOLIS.

8

BAS-RELIEF
IN ALABASTER
BRITISH
MUSEUM.

ASSYRIAN ORNAMENT.

The early history of Babylonia and Assyria is one long series of wars and conquests. Originally one nation, they became divided, and the younger Assyria in the north became the most powerful empire of that period, under Tiglath-Pileser I., B.C. 1100, Ashur-nasir-pal, B.C. 885-60, Shalmaneser II., B.C. 860-25, Tiglath-Pileser III., B.C. 745-27, the Great Sargon, B.C. 722-705, Sennacherib, B.C. 705-681, Esarhaddon, B.C. 681-668, and Ashur-ban-pal, B.C. 668-626. In B.C. 609 the capital, Nineveh, was destroyed by Cyaxares the Mede, and Babylon arose again to power under Nebuchadnezzar, B.C. 604-562 : this city was destroyed by Cyrus the Persian, B.C. 539.

Assyrian art, with its racial influences, religious beliefs, and climatic conditions, differs in a remarkable degree from Egyptian art. Though stone is found in Assyria, the great cities were built of brick, no doubt owing to the fact of the arts and civilization coming from Chaldea, where stone was scarce and clay plentiful. Both at Babylon in Chaldea and Nineveh in Assyria the traditional type of building was rectangular, with arched openings and vaults, built of sun-dried bricks. The lower part of the wall was covered with large alabaster slabs, carved in low relief with scenes representing the king and his warriors engaged in hunting or fighting (fig. 1). The upper part of the wall was in enamelled brick, or in coloured stucco, with details of the Lotus and the bud, together with the rosette, which was often carried round the archivolt. The representation of the industrial arts and the pursuits of agriculture, which is so admirably illustrated upon the Egyptian reliefs, is entirely absent in Assyria. The enamelled bricks of Chaldea were modelled in low relief, with enamels of turquoise blue, yellow, white, and black, of fine quality and colour—one splendid example is the Frieze of Archers from the Palace of Susa. The enamelled bricks of Assyria were usually flat, or modelled but slightly, and the enamels were less pure. The external walls were similar to the internal ones, but with larger friezes and bolder reliefs, and usually with religious subjects (fig. 9). The portals were enriched with colossal winged and human-headed bulls, of alabaster, finely carved in relief. Typical examples of Assyrian ornament are the Lotus and the bud (figs. 2 and 3), the Patera or Rosette (figs. 6 and 7), and the Hom, or Tree of Life (fig. 8). The Lotus enrichment shows Egyptian influence, and only came into use during the 7th century B.C., when intercourse between the two nations was established. It is differentiated from the Egyptian Lotus by its vigorous growth and curved profile, and the geometrical form of the calyx of the flower and bud (fig. 2).

The Anthemion or *Hom*, with its alternate bud and fir-cone, and with strong lateral markings, is beautiful in line and proportion of mass (fig. 3). The *Hom* is frequently used as a flower on the sacred tree, a form of enrichment that influenced much of the later Persian and Sicilian textile fabrics.

7

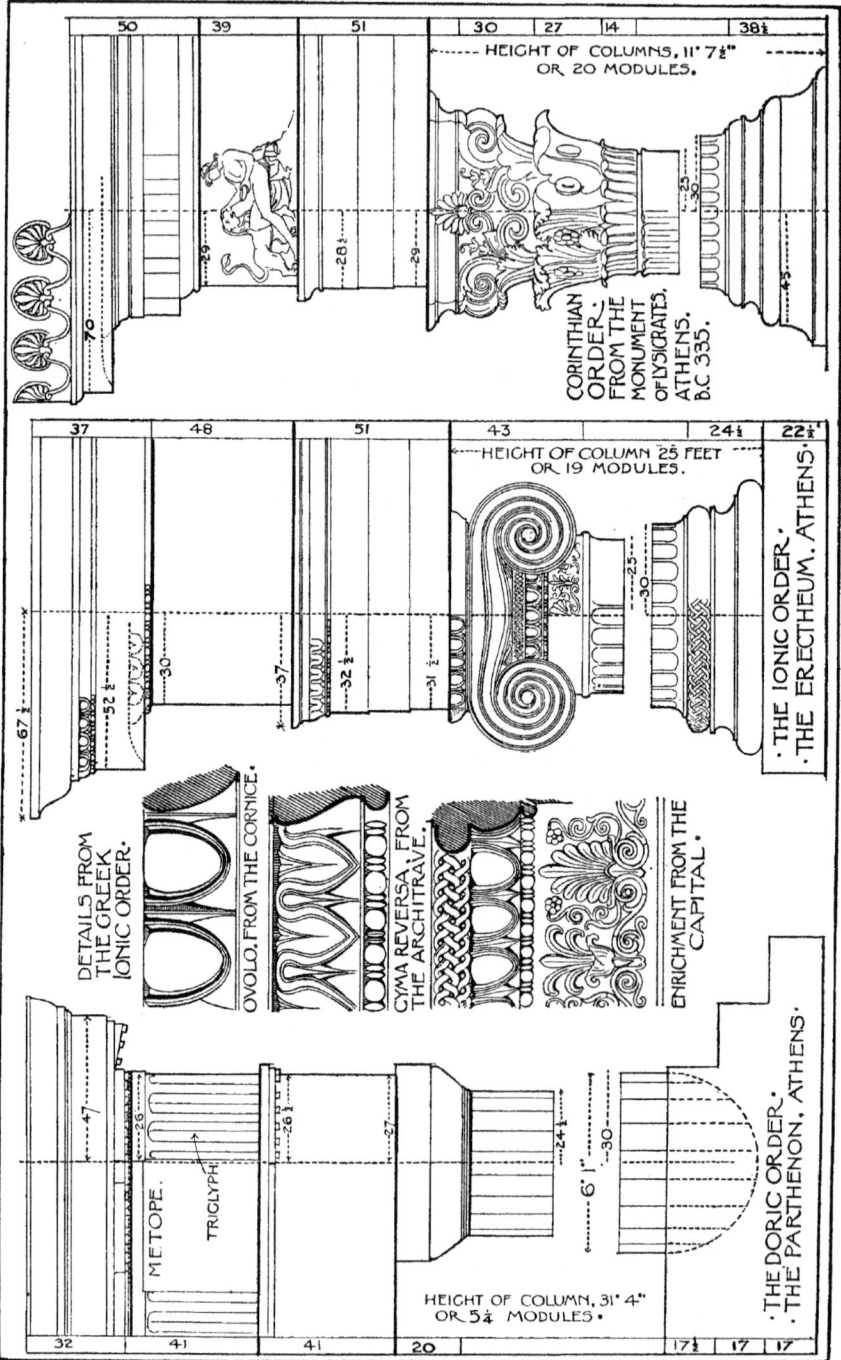

HEIGHT OF COLUMNS, 11' 7½"
OR 20 MODULES.

CORINTHIAN ORDER. FROM THE MONUMENT OF LYSICRATES. ATHENS. B.C. 335.

HEIGHT OF COLUMN 25 FEET OR 19 MODULES.

·THE IONIC ORDER· ·THE ERECTHEUM. ATHENS·

DETAILS FROM THE GREEK IONIC ORDER·

OVOLO, FROM THE CORNICE.

CYMA REVERSA. FROM THE ARCHITRAVE.

ENRICHMENT FROM THE CAPITAL·

METOPE.

TRIGLYPH.

·THE DORIC ORDER· ·THE PARTHENON, ATHENS·

HEIGHT OF COLUMN, 31' 4" OR 5¼ MODULES·

GREEK ARCHITECTURE.

Classic or columnar architecture is divided into the Greek and Roman styles, and each style comprises several orders of architecture: the Grecian orders are the Doric, the Ionic, and the Corinthian, and many examples of each of these orders are still extant in Greece and her colonies—Asia Minor, Southern Italy, and Sicily. From a comparison of these buildings, certain constructive and decorative features are observed to be present, and thence they are considered as the characteristics of the style or order, which comprises the base (except in the Grecian Doric, which has no base), column and capital, and the Entablature, which consists of the Architrave, Frieze, and Cornice. The proportions of these orders are generally determined by the lower diameter of the column, which is divided into 2 modules or 60 parts, the height of the column always including the base and capital. The DORIC order was used for the early Greek temples from B.C. 600, and culminated in the Parthenon, B.C. 438. The COLUMNS in this order are 4½ to 6 diameters in height, with 20 shallow flutings with intermediate sharp arrises; the CAPITAL is half a diameter in height, and is composed of an echinus or ovolo moulding with annulets or deep channellings below, and a large square abacus above. The ARCHITRAVE is plain; the FRIEZE is enriched by rectangular blocks, with 3 vertical channellings in the face, termed triglyths, alternately with square metopes which were frequently sculptured. The CORNICE, composed of simple mouldings, projects considerably beyond the face of the frieze.

CARYATIDE, ERECHTHEUM.

The IONIC order has columns of from 9 to 9½ diameters in height, with 24 flutings divided by narrow fillets; the *base* is half a diameter in height, and composed of a plinth, torus, fillet, cavetto, fillet, torus, and fillet. The CAPITAL is $\frac{7}{10}$ of a diameter high, and consists of a pair of double scrolls or volutes, supported by an echinus moulding enriched with the egg and tongue, with an astragal below.

The ENTABLATURE is one quarter the height of the columns, the ARCHITRAVE of one or more fascias, the FRIEZE continuous and frequently enriched with sculpture in low relief; the CORNICE has simple and compound mouldings supported by a dentil band. Caryatides were occasionally introduced into this order; they were female figures clad in drapery having vertical folds which re-echoed the flutings of the Ionic column. These Caryatides supported the entablature in place of the columns; a beautiful example is in the south portico of the Erechtheum at Athens.

9

The CORINTHIAN order was not much used by the Greeks; the examples, however, show considerable refinement and delicacy of details. The COLUMNS are 10 diameters in height, with 24 flutings; the BASE is half a diameter high; the CAPITAL is a little greater than a diameter in height, and is enriched with acanthus foliations and spiral volutes. The ENTABLATURE is richer and the CORNICE deeper and more elaborate than those of the other orders.

The principal Doric buildings in Greece are:—The Temples at Corinth[2,8], B.C. 650, Ægina[2,8], B.C. 550, the Parthenon[2,9], and the Theseum[2,8], B.C. 438; the Temples of Jupiter at Olympia[2,8], B.C. 436, Apollo Epicurius at Bassæ[2,8], B.C. 436, Propylæa at Athens, B.C. 431, and the Minerva at Sunium, B.C. 420. Ionic buildings are:— Temples at Ilyssus[1,7], B.C. 484, Nike Apteros[1,7], B.C. 420, and the Erechtheum, B.C. 420 (see plan, plate 54), North Portico[7], East Portico[8], at Athens. In Asia Minor there are the Temples of Samos[8], Priene[8], Teos[8], Diana at Ephesus[9] (with 36 of its columns sculptured), and of Apollo at Miletos. Corinthian buildings are:— The Monument of Lysicrates, B.C. 335, the Tower of the Winds (octagonal in plan), and Jupiter Olympius[2,8], B.C. 200.

During the 5th century B.C. the Doric order was extensively used in the Greek colonies at Sicily. At Agrigentum there are the remains of six fine Doric temples, of which the Temple of Zeus[2], B.C. 450, is the largest, being 354 by 175 ft. In this Temple were found the *Telemones*, or *Atlantes*, male figures, 25 ft. in height, with their arms raised, probably supporting the roof. This Temple is also remarkable for its portico of seven columns, 60 ft. in height, and having the peristyle walled up.

At Selinus there are five large Doric temples[2,8], and one[5,9] with columns 57 ft. in height, with an entablature of 19 ft. At Segesta there is a Doric temple[2,8] with only the peristyle complete and the columns unfluted, and at Pæstum, in southern Italy, there are two Doric temples[2,8] and a basilica[5] with its porticos of nine columns each.

All these buildings in Sicily and Pæstum date between 500 and 430 B.C.

CLASSIFICATION OF CLASSIC TEMPLES.

ARRANGEMENT OF COLUMNS AND WALLS.

[1] *Apteral*	-	When the side walls have no colonnade.
[2] *Peripteral*	-	When there is a colonnade standing apart from the side walls.
[3] *Pseudo-peripteral*		When the colonnade is attached to the side walls.
[4] *Dipteral*	-	When there is a double colonnade standing out from the walls.
[5] *Pseudo-dipteral*	-	When the inner row of columns are attached to the side walls.

THE RELATION OF THE ENDS OF THE TEMPLE.

In Antis	-	When the columns do not project beyond the ends of the side walls.
Prostyle	-	When a portico stands in front of the temple.
[6] *Amphi-prostyle*	-	When there is a portico at each end.
Mono-prostyle	-	If the portico is one column in depth.
Di-prostyle	-	If the portico is two columns in depth.

THE NUMBER OF COLUMNS IN THE PORTICO.

[7] *Tetrastyle*	-	If of four columns.
[8] *Hexastyle*	-	If of six columns.
[9] *Octastyle*	-	If of eight columns.

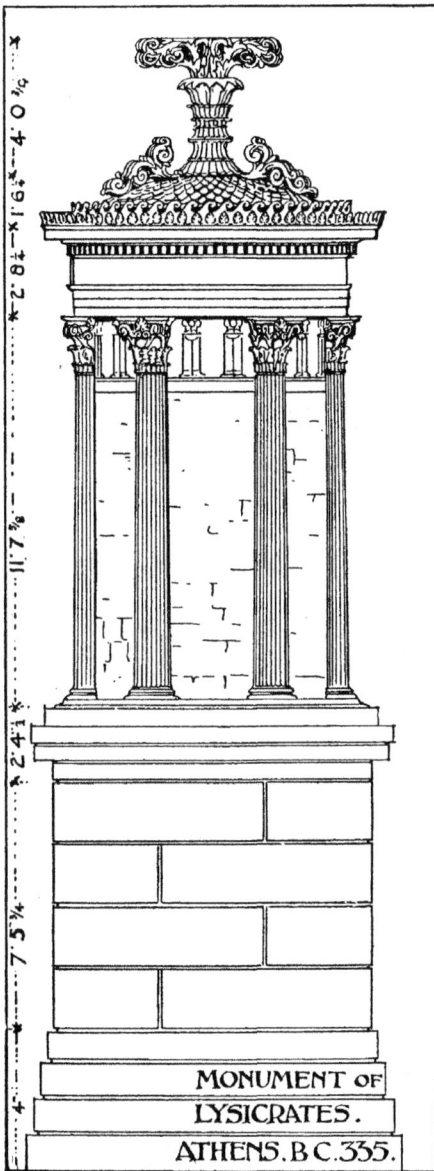

MONUMENT OF LYSICRATES. ATHENS. B.C. 335.

PROPORTIONS OF THE ENTABLATURE, IN PARTS.

		Archi-trave.	Frieze.	Cor-nice.	Total Enta-blature.
DORIC -	Parthenon -	44½	40½	26	111
	Theseus -	50	55½	25½	131
IONIC -	Erechtheum	51½	48½	37½	137½
	Priene -	46⅔	29	55⅔	131½
CORINTHIAN	Lysicrates -	51	39½	50	140½
	Jupiter Olympius	41⅔	27⅓	48	117

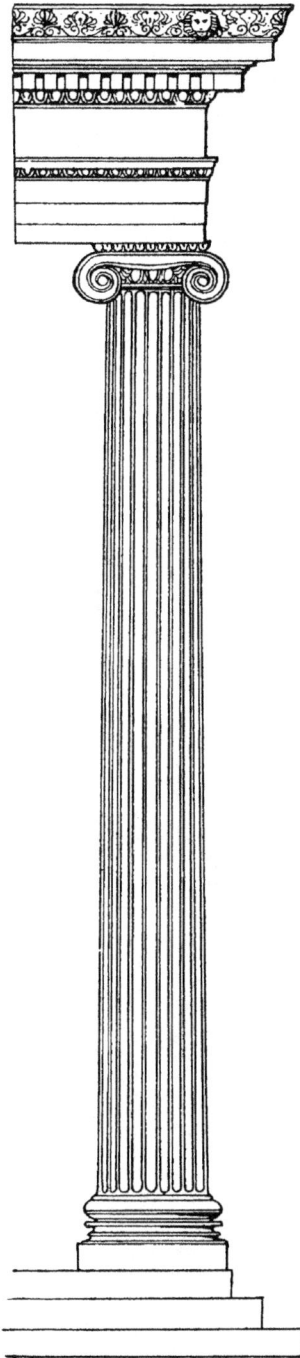

IONIC ORDER, TEMPLE OF ILYSSUS.

II

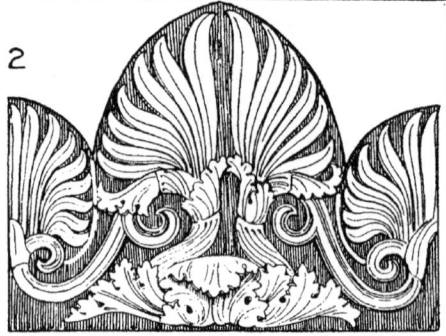

ANTHEMION ORNAMENT FROM GREEK TOMBS. ATHENS. B.C. 360

ORNAMENT FROM THE MONUMENT OF
LYSICRATES. ATHENS
B.C. 330.

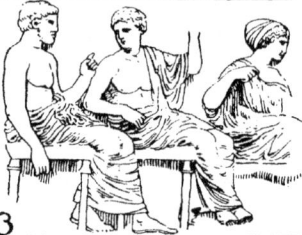

FIGURES FROM THE EAST FRIEZE
OF THE PARTHENON
B.C. 438.

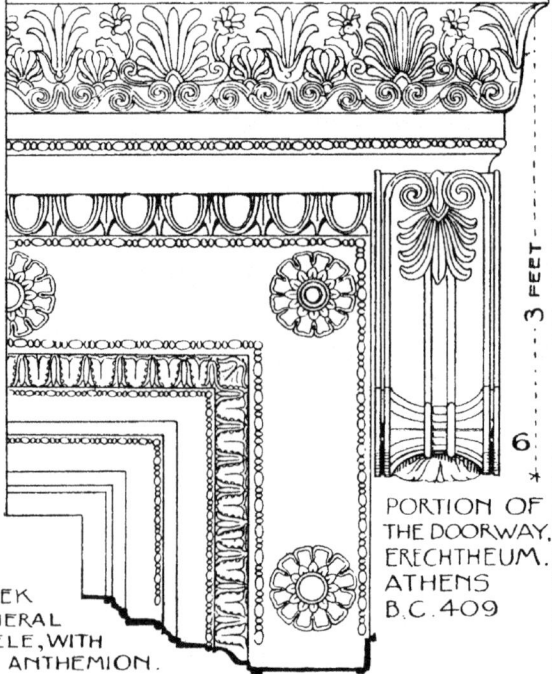

GREEK
FUNERAL
STELE, WITH
THE ANTHEMION.

3 FEET

PORTION OF
THE DOORWAY,
ERECHTHEUM.
ATHENS
B.C. 409

GREEK ORNAMENT.

Greece, or Hellas, consisted of a number of small states, speaking the same language, and worshipping the same gods. Almost the whole of the Ægean coast of Asia Minor was occupied in early times by Greek Colonies, which supplanted those of the Phœnicians of Tyre and Sidon. The southern portion of this seaboard was occupied by the Dorians, and the northern by Ionians. In the course of time other Greek settlements were made on the Black Sea and Mediterranean Coast of Asia Minor, as well as at Syracuse, Gela and Agrigentum in Sicily, and in Etruria and Magna Grecia in Italy. These colonies appear to have reached a higher state of art at an early period than Greece itself. The ascendency in art in Greece was enjoyed by the Dorians circa, 800 B.C.; after which Sparta took the lead, but was in turn excelled by the Ionians, when Athens became the focus of Greek art, and attained a degree of perfection in that respect that has remained unequalled to this day. Athens was destroyed by the Persians under Xerxes, 480 B.C.; but under Pericles (470-429 B.C.) Greek art reached its culmination.

The abundant, although fragmentary, remains of Grecian architecture, sculpture, and the industrial arts, show most vividly the artistic feeling and culture of the early Greeks, with their great personality and religious sentiment, in which the personal interest of the gods and goddesses was brought into relation with the life and customs of the people. Their myths and traditions, their worship of legendary heroes, the perfection of their physical nature, and their intense love of the beautiful, were characteristic of the Greek people, from the siege of Troy to their subjection by Rome, B.C. 140. The almost inexhaustible store of Greek art, now gathered in the British Museum, and in other European museums, furnishes one of the most valuable illustrations of the many glorious traditions of the past. The vitality of conception, the dignity and noble grace of the gods, the consummate knowledge of the human figure, and the exquisite skill of craftmanship, are here seen in the greatest diversity of treatment and incident.

The work of Phidias, the most renowned of Greek sculptors, is largely represented in the British Museum by noble examples, showing his great personality, wonderful power, and his remarkable influence upon contemporary and later plastic art.

The Parthenon, or temple of the goddess Athene, which was built upon the Acropolis at Athens by Ictinus and Callicrates, B.C. 454-438, was enriched with splendid works of sculpture by Phidias. Many of the originals are now in the British Museum forming part of the Elgin Marbles, which were purchased from the Earl of Elgin, in 1815. The two pediments of the temple contained figure sculpture in the round, larger than life size. The Eastern group represents the birth of Athene, and the western group the contest of Athene and Poseidon

13

WIDTH 101 FEET

for the soil of Attica. The fragments of these pedimental groups are now in the British Museum, and, though sadly mutilated, show the perfection of sculpture during the Phidian age. Of the 92 square metopes sculptured in high relief, that enriched the Doric frieze, 15 are included in the Elgin Marbles. The subject represented on these metopes was the battle between the Centaurs and Lapithæ, or Greéks, —a fine example of composition of line and mass, and dramatic power of expression.

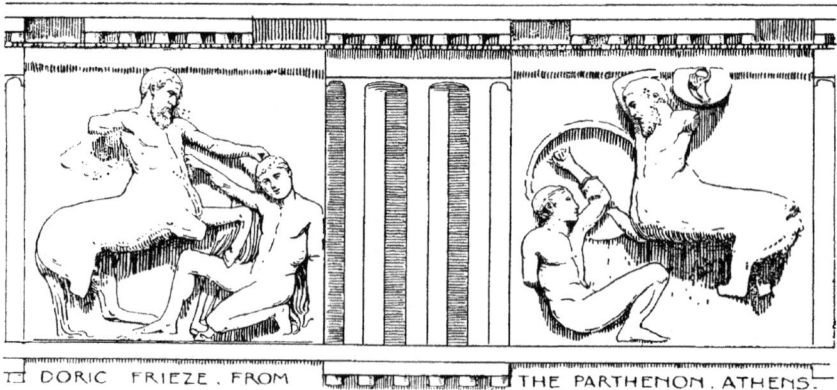

DORIC FRIEZE . FROM   THE PARTHENON . ATHENS.

The continuous frieze upon the upper part of the cella wall, under the colonnade or Peristyle, was 40 feet from the ground, 40 inches in height, and 523 feet in length. It was carved in low relief, the subject being the Panathenæic procession, the most sacred and splendid of the religious festivals of the Ancient Greeks. This frieze, with its rhythm of movement and unity of composition, its groups of beautiful youths and maidens, sons and daughters of noble citizens,

14

its heroes and deities, heralds and magistrates; its sacrificial oxen, and its horses and riders are doubtless the most perfect production of the sculptor's art. Each figure is full of life and motion, admirable in detail, having an individuality of action and expression, yet with a unity of composition, appropriate to its architectural purpose as a frieze or band.

NORTH FRIEZE FROM THE PARTHENON ATHENS

The Parthenon, however, was but the shrine of the standing figure or statue of the goddess Athene, which was 37 feet high, and formed of plates of gold and ivory, termed *Chryselephantine* sculpture. Probably owing to the intrinsic value of the material, this work of Phidias disappeared at an early date.

Among the examples of sculptured marbles in the British Museum is the beautiful frieze from the interior of the Temple of Apollo at Phigaleia, erected by Ictinus, B.C. 450-430. This frieze, which shows an extraordinary vitality and movement, is 101 feet long and consists of 23 slabs 25½ inches in width, the incidents depicted being the battle of the Greeks and the Amazons, and the contest between the Centaurs and the Lapithæ. The dignity and reserve of the Parthenon frieze is here replaced by activity and energy of line and an exuberance of modelling.

BATTLE OF THE AMAZONS. FROM THE FRIEZE AT PHIGALEIA

Some of the marbles in the British Museum are from the Nereid Monument of Xanthos, B.C. 372, so called because the female figures display moist clinging garments, and have fishes and seabirds between

15

their feet. These sculptures show a high degree of perfection, and were probably the work of the Athenian sculptor, Bryaxis.

Among other examples of the Greek treatment of the frieze, is that of the Erectheum, B.C. 409, with its black Eleusinian stone background, and white marble reliefs. The Temple of Nike Apteros, of about the same date, is noted for the beautiful reliefs from the balustrade which crowned the lofty bastion on which the temple stands. An example of Nike or victory, adjusting her sandal, is here given. These reliefs are remarkable for their delicacy and refinement of treatment, and the exquisite rendering of the draped female figure. Other friezes now in the British Museum are from the Mausoleum erected by Artemisia to her husband, Mausolus, B.C. 357-348. This tomb consisted of a solid basement of masonry, supporting a cella surrounded by a colonnade of 36 columns. The upper part of the basement was enriched with a frieze illustrating the battle of the Centaurs and Lapithæ ; the frieze of the cella was illustrated with funeral games in honour of Mausolus. Seventeen slabs of the frieze of the order from the colonnade are in the British Museum ; they represent the battle of the Greeks and Amazons. In their composition these slabs show extraordinary energy of movement and richness of invention. This frieze differs absolutely from the Parthenon frieze in its fertility of incident and intensity of action. Bryaxis, the sculptor of the Nereid monument executed the north frieze, while the south was by Timotheus, the east by Scopas, and the west by Leochares.

BAS-RELIEF FROM NIKE APTEROS.

A remarkable building, where again the frieze was an important feature, was the great altar at Pergamos, erected by Eumenes II., B.C. 168. This had a basement of masonry 160 ft. by 160 ft., and 16 ft. high, enriched with a sculptured frieze 7½ ft. high. The subject is the *Gigantomachia*, or battle of the gods and giants ; the treatment being characterised by passionate energy and expression, and daring skill in grouping and technique. Ninety-four of the original slabs of this frieze are now in the Berlin Museum.

The frieze was an important decorative feature with the Assyrians and Greeks. The continuity of incident and rhythm of movement that was possible with the continuous frieze, together with its functional use of banding, no doubt tended to preserve its traditional form, hence we have many remains from antiquity of this beautiful decorative treatment. An early and fine example is the frieze of Archers from the palace of Susa, B.C. 485, now in the Louvre. This frieze, of which an illustration is here given, was executed in glazed and enamelled bricks. A dignity of conception and unity of composition were here combined with skilful modelling of relief work, and fine colouring of blue, turquoise and yellow. This treatment of the frieze no doubt influenced the later work of the Greeks, who so nobly carried on this tradition of the frieze.

FRIEZE IN ENAMELLED BRICKS FROM THE PALACE OF SUSA 485 B.C. LOUVRE

Greek ornament is distinguished by simplicity of line, refinement of detail, radiation of parts, unity of composition, and perfect symmetry. The anthemion, which is the typical form, is derived from the traditional lotus and bud of Egypt, Assyria, and India. It differs, however, in its more abstract rendering and its absence of symbolism, having a charm of composition and a unity and balance of parts, yet lacking that interest and deeper significance associated with many periods of art.

The anthemion was sculptured upon the top of the funeral stele (figs. 1, 2, and 5, plate 5), upon the architrave of doorways (fig. 6), and above the necking of the Ionic columns (plate 4), or painted upon the panels of the deep coffered ceilings. It was also used in a thousand ways upon the many fine vases and other ceramic wares of that period. The simplicity and beauty of the anthemion and its ready adaptability, has doubtless rendered it one of the best known types of ornament. Like the Egyptian and Assyrian prototype, the Greek anthemion is usually arranged with alternate flower and bud, connected by a curved line or more frequently by a double spiral. Illustrations are given on plate 6 of a few typical examples, where the rhythm and beauty of composition are indicative of the culture and perfection of Greek craftsmanship.

Another feature, which at a later period received considerable

EXAMPLES OF BANDS FROM GREEK VASES. OWEN JONES.

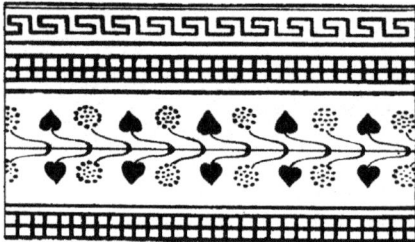

FROM THE MUSEUM NAPLES

ORNAMENT IN MARBLE, FROM THE ROOF APEX. MONUMENT OF LYSICRATES. ATHENS. B.C. 335

development, was the scroll given on plate 6, which is a fine example from the roof of the monument to Lysicrates. The scrolls, cut with V-shaped sections, spring from a nest of sharp acanthus foliage. This scroll is formed of a series of spirals springing from each other, the junction of the spiral being covered by a sheath or flower ; the spiral itself being often broken by a similar sheath.

This spiral form, with its sheathing, is the basis of the Roman and Italian Renascence styles, and sharply differentiates them from the Gothic ornament, in which the construction line is continuous and unbroken.

The rosette, a survival of the traditional Assyrian form, was frequently used upon the Architrave (fig. 6), and the funeral stele (fig. 5, plate 5) where its circular and radiating form contrasts so beautifully with the functional straight lines of architectural design. The extraordinary vitality and versatility of the Greek craftsmen may be traced through a magnificent series of coins dating from B.C. 700 to B.C. 280. The interest of subject, beauty of composition and largeness of style, combined with the utmost delicacy of technique, of these gold, silver, and electrum coins, are a reflex of the artistic feeling for beauty of the early Greeks.

COIN OF PHILIP II. B.C. 339-336. COIN OF TERINA B.C. 412. COIN OF AGRIGENTUM B.C. 412-406

Colour, as well as form, was a great factor in the art of the Greeks; their architecture and sculpture were enriched and accentuated by the judicious use of beautiful colour. The Parthenon, with its simple and refined Doric architecture, and magnificent sculpture by Phidias, was enhanced by colour, which was introduced in the background of the pediment and the frieze, and also upon the borders and accessories of the draperies. The " Lacunaria," or sunk panels of the ceilings, were frequently enhanced with blue, having rosettes or stars in gold or colour. A frank use of pure colour was almost universal in early Egyptian and Assyrian art, and the Greeks were not slow to avail themselves of any art that was beautiful.

19

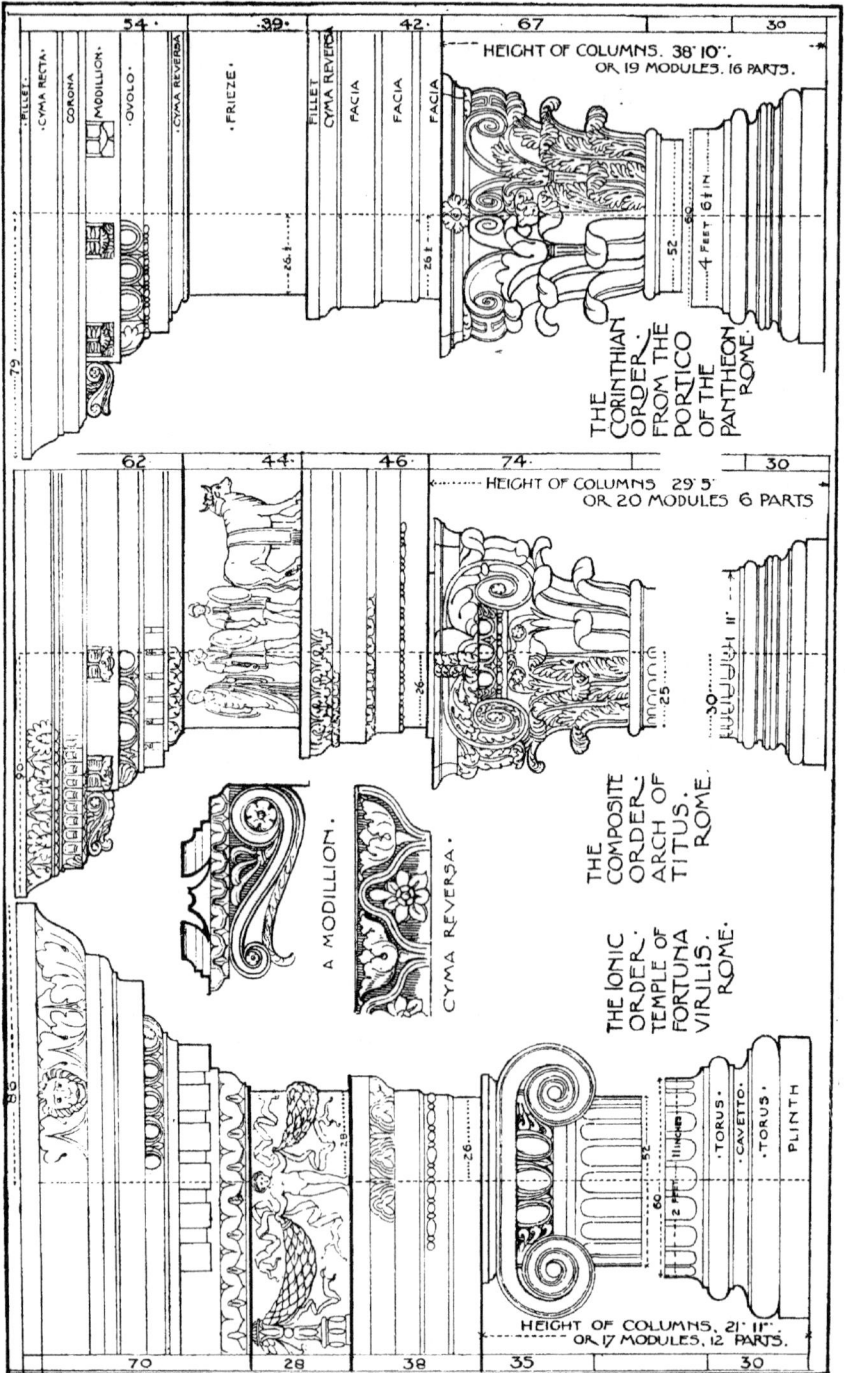

THE CORINTHIAN ORDER. FROM THE PORTICO OF THE PANTHEON. ROME.

HEIGHT OF COLUMNS. 38'·10". OR 19 MODULES. 16 PARTS.

54 · · 39· 42 · 67 30

FILLET · CYMA RECTA · CORONA · MODILLION · OVOLO · CYMA REVERSA · FRIEZE · FILLET CYMA REVERSA · FACIA · FACIA · FACIA ·

4 FEET · 6¼ IN.

THE COMPOSITE ORDER· ARCH OF TITUS. ROME.

HEIGHT OF COLUMNS 29'·5" OR 20 MODULES 6 PARTS

62 44· 46 · 74 · 30

A MODILLION.

CYMA REVERSA ·

THE IONIC ORDER· TEMPLE OF FORTUNA VIRILIS. ROME.

· TORUS · CAVETTO · TORUS · PLINTH

HEIGHT OF COLUMNS. 21'·11". OR 17 MODULES, 12 PARTS.

70 28 38 35 30

ROMAN ARCHITECTURE

Is differentiated from that of Greece by the extensive use of the arch and of superposed orders. The many fine remains of Roman temples and public buildings show the extraordinary versatility and conception of the Roman architects, their constructive skill, and their remarkable power of assimilating the arts of other nations. The Roman temples were somewhat similar in plan to their Greek prototypes, but usually without the side colonnade, larger in scale, and with an ostentatious display of mouldings and ornaments, less refined in contour and detail.

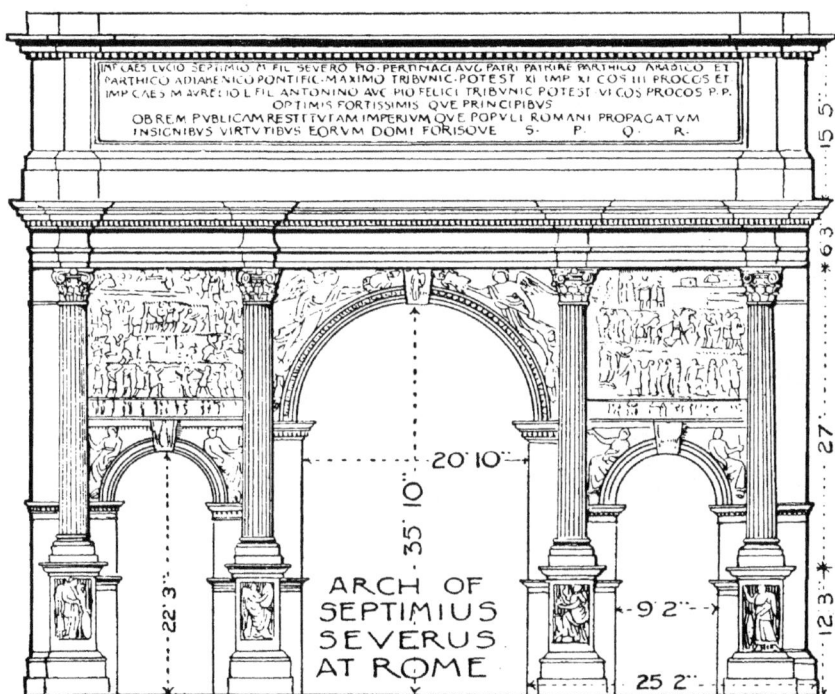

INP CAES LVCIO SEPTIMIO M FIL SEVERO PIO·PERTINACI AVG PATRI PATRIAE PARTHICO ARABICO ET
PARTHICO ADIABENICO PONTIFIC·MAXIMO TRIBVNIC·POTEST XI IMP XI COS III PROCOS ET
IMP CAES M AVRELIO L FIL ANTONINO AVG PIO FELICI TRIBVNIC POTEST VI COS PROCOS P·P·
OPTIMIS FORTISSIMIS QVE PRINCIPIBVS
OB REM PVBLICAM RESTITVTAM IMPERIVM QVE POPVLI ROMANI PROPAGATVM
INSIGNIBVS VIRTVTIBVS EORVM DOMI FORISQVE   S·   P·   Q·   R·

ARCH OF SEPTIMIUS SEVERUS AT ROME

A typical example is given here of a triumphal arch, namely, that of Septimus Severus, A.D. 203. Other examples are the Arch of Titus, A.D. 83, and the Arch of Constantine, A.D. 326, all near the Forum at Rome. Trajan's Arch, A.D. 114, was destroyed by Constantine, who used many of the reliefs for the building of his own arch.

The superposition of columns and arches is seen in the Theatre of Marcellus, B.C. 20, where the lower order is of the Doric and the upper of the Ionic, and, like the early Greek Theatre, was semi-circular in plan.

The Colosseum, commenced by Vespasian, A.D. 72, and completed

21

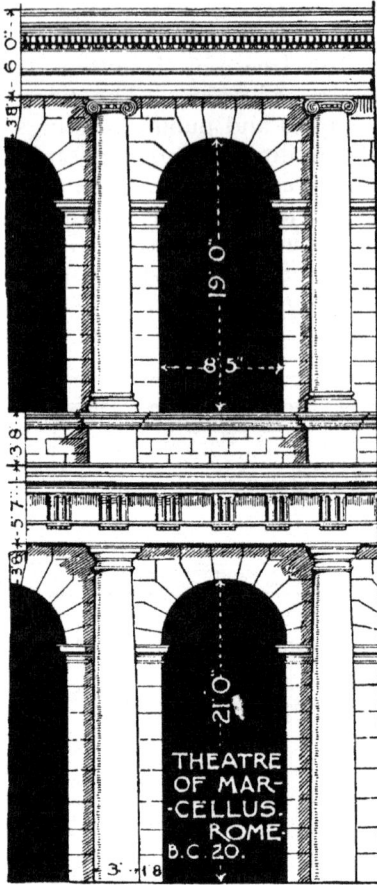

THEATRE
OF MAR-
-CELLUS.
ROME.
B.C. 20.

by Titus, A.D. 80, has a third story, having the Corinthian order, and an attic story, with Corinthian pilasters, the whole reaching to a height of 157 ft. The diameter of the amphitheatre was 584 by 468 ft.

One of the best preserved buildings of the early Roman period is the Pantheon (plan, plate 54), built during the reign of Hadrian, A.D. 118-38. This has a fine dome of coffered panels, having a diameter of 142 ft., and an altitude of 71 ft. 6 in., with a total height of 143 ft. from the floor to eye of dome.

The beautiful octastyle Corinthian portico, of the time of Agrippa, B.C. 27, has granite columns 46 ft. 6 in. in height, with fine capitals in white marble.

The magnificent temple of Castor and Pollux, frequently called Jupiter Stator, is only known from the three columns still standing; but these show the magnitude of scale and the exuberance of detail that characterized the finest period of Roman architecture. The proportions of this order are columns, 45 ft. 3 in. in height and the entablature 11 ft. 7 in.

The Tuscan and Composite orders were added to the Doric, Ionic, and Corinthian orders, thus forming the five orders of architecture.

The Romans rarely used the peristyle temple, consequently the cella was of the same width as the portico. In the civic buildings and palaces, the Romans show the greatest constructive skill

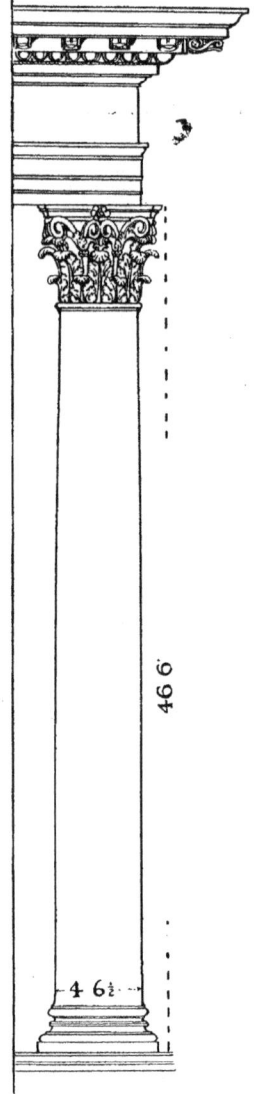

THE CORINTHIAN ORDER
FROM THE PANTHEON

22

and splendour of embellishment. The skilful planning and appropriateness of decorative treatment in their basilicas and amphitheatres are evidences of the practical nature of the Romans.

The Basilica or Hall of Justice was an important architectural feature, rectangular in plan, with a semi-circular apse at one end, where the Tribunal was placed; roofed with timber framing, or vaulted with concrete, and supported with rows of columns or piers. The remains of two typical Roman basilicas are still in existence: the Basilica of Trajan, A.D. 114, rectangular, 180 by 160 ft., five aisles, the centre aisle with a semi-circular wooden roof, and enriched with bronze plates, is typical of one class ; and the Basilica of Maxentinus, A.D. 310, with a width of 195 ft., and a length of 260 ft., is typical of a vaulted Basilica, the two side aisles with an arched roof, and the centre aisle with an intersecting vaulted roof.

These Roman basilicas were adopted by the early Christians to their service, and the basilica church became the typical form used up to the 12th century in the Romanesque provinces.

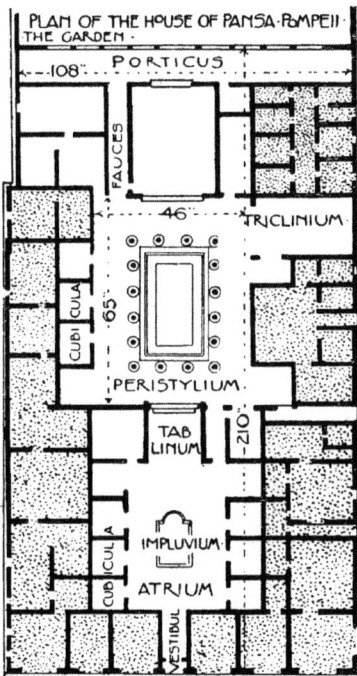

PLAN OF THE HOUSE OF PANSA·POMPEII.
THE GARDEN·
PORTICUS
108
FAUCES
46
TRICLINIUM
CUBICULA
65
PERISTYLIUM·
TABLINUM
210
CUBICULA
IMPLUVIUM
ATRIUM
VESTIBUL

The Roman houses were of two types: the *Domus*, or houses clustered together, and the *Insular*, houses which were surrounded by streets. Most of the finest Pompeian houses were of the *Insular* type.

The usual plan of a Roman house consisted of the *Ostium*, an entrance or *Vestibule*, which opened into the *Atrium*, a large room or court partly roofed over, with an opening in the centre called the *Conpluvium*, under which was the *Impluvium*, or cistern of water, placed below the level of the ground. Small chambers surrounded the *Atrium*, and at the further end was the *Tablinum* or private room, frequently leading to the *Peristylium* or private part of the house, an open court, with a colonnade surrounding a marble fountain, with flowers, shrubs, and trees, forming a *Viridarium*. Surrounding the *Peristylium* were private rooms, one of which was the *Triclinium*, or dining room. From the *Peristylium*, *fauces* or passages led to the *Porticus*, a colonnade which overlooked the garden.

23

FIG 1

42 INCHES

FRIEZE. FORUM OF TRAJAN. LATERAN MUSEUM.

2

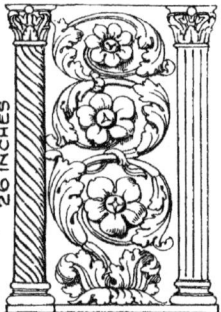

26 INCHES

ONE SIDE OF A SQUARE
SEPULCHRAL CIPPUS

3

15 INCHES

ROMAN SCROLL

14½

4 & 5

MARBLE
PANELS·
BRITISH
MUSEUM·

14½

6

PANEL OF VOTIVE CIPPIUS

8

7

32 INCHES

TRIANGULAR BASE OF A MARBLE
CANDELABRUM. BRITISH MUSEUM

38 INCHES

FRIEZE. FORUM OF TRAJAN. ROME 110 A.D

ROMAN ORNAMENT.

Rome, founded by Romulus, B.C. 783, became by successive wars and conquests the mistress of the world, absorbing the arts and the architecture of the Etruscans B.C. 567, the Samnites B.C. 340, and of Corinth and Carthage B.C. 146. From these varied sources arose the style termed Roman, assimilating and adopting the column and the horizontal entablature of the Greeks ; the arch, the vault, the mural paintings, and the decorative use of bronze and terra-cotta of the Etruscans, with the sculpture, ornament, mosaics and coinage of the Greeks and Carthaginians. These varied arts were assimilated and perfected by the Romans during the period B.C. 100 to 337 A.D.

Roman ornament is the continuity of the Greek and Etruscan styles, consisting of the anthemion, the acanthus and the scroll ; the Romans using these forms with greater exuberance and elaboration, together with bold and vigorous carving, yet lacking the simplicity, refinement, and graceful contour of the Greek and Etruscan forms.

Roman ornament consists largely of continuous spiral lines, clothed with cups and sheaths of acanthus foliage, the various spirals terminating in a rosette. These main spirals are frequently interwoven with fine curved or spiral lines, clothed with acanthus or other foliation, such as the vine, olive and ivy. Birds and reptiles and cupids, and the chimera or griffin (fig. 1) are often interspersed with the ornament, thus giving that largeness of mass, and contrast of form, which is so characteristic of Roman art. The Thermæ, or baths and public buildings, displayed fine decorative ceilings, having deep sunk panels called Lacunaria, or coffers ; square, hexagonal or octagonal in form, with a centre rosette in high relief and the border mouldings of

COFFERED CEILING TEMPLE OF PEACE. ROME

the coffers being enriched with the egg and dart, or the water leaf. These exhibit an effective treatment of moulded surfaces. The ceilings of the tombs and palaces were in many cases ornamented

FIG. 1

3

MARBLE RELIEF IN THE UFFIZI GALLERY.
FLORENCE.

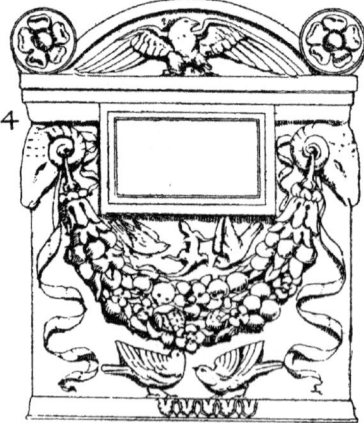

STUCCO
DECORATION IN LOW RELIEF.
REPRESENTING NYMPHS RIDING ON WINGED
& SEA MONSTERS & NEREIDS SURROUNDED
WITH ORNAMENT. FROM A TOMB ON THE
VIA LATINA ROME. A.D 160. DISCOVERED IN 1860.
THE CEILING IS BARREL-VAULTED & ORNAMENTED
SEE FIG 2.

2

STUCCO ORNAMENT IN LOW RELIEF UPON A CEILING IN TOMB VIA LATINA
ROME.

5

RELIEF PANEL FROM THE INSIDE OF THE PORTICO OF THE
PANTHEON. ROME. A.D. 125.

4

6

CINERARY URN. BRITISH MUSEUM.

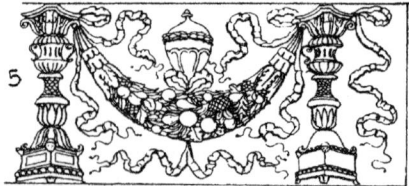

MARBLE URN. BRITISH MUSEUM.

with circular and square panels, richly decorated with arabesques or mythical figures, and cupids in low relief of fine stucco ; the mouldings or divisions in higher relief, and having the water leaf or the egg and dart enrichment (plate 9).

The architectural frieze and the sepulchral urn and sarcophagi of this period were often decorated with festoons (figs. 4 and 5, plate 9),

FRIEZE
TEMPLE OF VESTA TIVOLI

and which were supported by cupids or by candelabra (plate 9), or by the skulls of oxen, as on the frieze from the Temple of Vesta at Tivoli, here given, which is no doubt a survival of the sacrificial custom of worship.

The architectural basilica and forum of Trajan, erected A.D. 114, by Apollodorus, a Greek of Damascus, was of the utmost magnificence, the remains attesting to the skill and artistic craftsmanship of the Romans. Apollodorus also erected the marble column of Trajan, having a rectangular pedestal 18 feet high, and richly sculptured with the dresses, armour and standards of the Roman army. This pedestal supports a column of the Tuscan order of architecture $97\frac{1}{4}$ ft. high, and 12 ft. in diameter, enriched with a series of spiral bands, having bas-reliefs representing the successive events of the Dacian War by the Emperor Trajan.

This magnificent and well preserved relic of antiquity furnishes a complete epitome of the costumes and the arms and armour of that period. Another well preserved column, similar to that of Trajan, was erected in Rome by Marcus Aurelius, A.D. 174, the subjects of its reliefs being the war with the Marcomans. Large marble urns, or Tazzas, enriched with Bacchanalian figures, surrounded with foliage and birds and animals ; magnificent tables, chairs, couches, and candelabra, of bronze, enriched with silver damascening, together with the choice remains of sculpture and mosaics, all indicate the luxuriousness and love of magnificence of the wealthy Roman citizens.

In Roman architectural ornament we see the most powerful modelling combined with the use of the continuous scroll growing from a nest of foliage, repeated in their painted decorations (see Pompeian). This elaboration of the typical Greek ornamentation and the rounded serrations of the Acanthus (see plate 33), forms the chief characteristic of Roman ornament, which is wonderfully bold and vigorous in conception and execution, but deficient in the refinement and delicacy of Greek art.

There is a considerable difference in the foliations of the various capitals. The Corinthian capital of the Parthenon has foliage of the simple olive leaf type. In the composite capital of the Arch of Septimus Severus the foliage is serrated like fig. 8, plate 8, while that of the Corinthian capital of the Temple of Vesta, Tivoli, is more of the parsley leaf type, and each leaf is folded forward at the terminations.

27

FRIEZE FROM THE TEMPLE OF ISIS.

RED GROUND

A PAINTED
PILLAR.

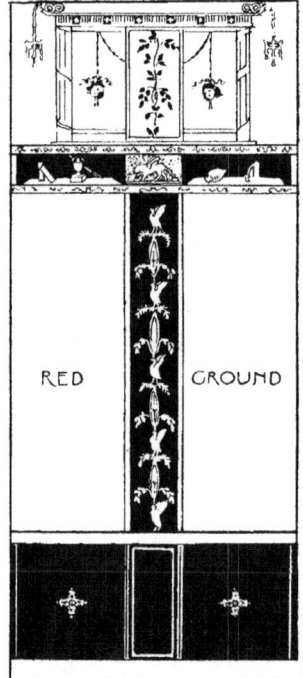

WALL DECORATION IN THE
CASA DEL LABIRINTO. POMPEII.

PAINTED PILASTER
FROM POMPEII.
ZAHNS POMPEII.

WALL DECORATION. FORUM OF
HERCULES. POMPEII. 79. A.D.

POMPEIAN ORNAMENT.

Pompeii, Herculaneum and Stabia, Roman cities, were buried by an eruption of Vesuvius, A.D. 79. These cities had already suffered from an earthquake, A.D. 63, and were being rapidly rebuilt when they were finally destroyed by the eruption. The Younger Pliny, the historian, was a spectator of the event at Pompeii, and wrote two letters to his friend Tacitus, describing the event and his flight from the doomed city, which remained buried for seventeen centuries, with the treasures of gold and silver, bronzes of rare workmanship, mural paintings on a most magnificent scale, and floors of mosaics of marvellous execution and design ; everything affording a vivid glimpse of the domestic and public life of the Romans of the 1st century A.D. Herculaneum was discovered in 1709, and Pompeii 1748, and from these cities many valuable remains of art have been taken. In the museum at Naples there are over 1,000 mural paintings, some 13,000 small bronzes, over 150 large bronzes of figures and busts, and 70 fine large mosaics.

A plan of a Roman house is given on page 23 showing the arrangement and use of the rooms. The floors covered with mosaics (see plate 33), those of the vestibule, corridors, and small rooms having simple patterns enclosed with borders of the key pattern, or the Guilloche in black, red, grey, and white tesseriæ. The floor of the triclinium, or dining room, was often a magnificent mosaic representing some mythological or classical subject. The walls were painted in colour, usually with a dado ⅙th the height of the wall, with pilasters dividing the wall into rectangular panels and a frieze above (plate 10). The general scheme of colour was, the dado and pilasters black, the panels red, and the frieze white ; or black dado, red pilasters and frieze, with white or yellow panels. The decorations upon these various coloured grounds was light and fanciful, and painted with great delicacy. Representations of architectural forms, such as columns and entablatures, are often rendered in perspective upon the painted walls.

The painted ornament has somewhat the same characteristics as the Roman relief work, but is usually much more delicate in treatment. The spiral form and the sheath are always prevalent, and from these sheaths and cups grow the finer tendrils or delicately painted spray of foliage, upon which birds are placed.

Stucco enrichments, such as ornamental string courses and mouldings, were frequently combined with the painted ornament ; they consist of small details, such as the water-leaf, the egg and dart, and the anthemion, and are repeated in a regular series.

Herculaneum differed considerably from Pompeii, for the finest works of art and innumerable MSS. have been found, shewing that a higher intellectual life existed than that at Pompeii, where not a single MS. has been found. It is probable that Herculaneum was equal to Athens itself in the wealth of its art treasures.

FROM
ST MARKS
VENICE.

LILY
CAPITAL.
ST MARKS.

CAPITAL
FROM SAN
VITALE.
RAVENNA

PIERCED
MARBLE
SCREEN.
ST MARKS.

SARCOPHAGI OF THEODSIUS. 7TH CENTURY. S. APOLLINARE. RAVENNA.

PIERCED MARBLE
SCREEN, ST MARKS.

FROM ST MARKS.

ANCIENT
PIER.
VENICE.

CARVED PANELS IN ALABASTER FROM ST MARKS. VENICE. 1071.

BYZANTINE ORNAMENT.

The decline of the Roman empire, in the 3rd and 4th centuries A.D., had its inevitable influence upon contemporary art, but perhaps a more potent influence was that of Christianity, which, under the reign of Constantine, received state recognition and support; and when this Emperor removed the seat of government from Rome to Byzantium, the traditional Greek and Roman arts were assimilated with those of Persia and Syria, but moulded and influenced by the new religion, giving that strong vitality, deep significance, and symbolism which is so remarkable a feature of the Byzantine style.

The change of style did not take place immediately, for most of the buildings erected by Constantine were in the traditional Roman style, but the arts were gradually perfected until they culminated in the building of S. Sophia, by Anthemius of Tralles and Isidorus of Miletus, during the reign of Justinian, A.D. 538. This building is remarkable for its splendid dome, supported by semi-domes and pendentives on a square plan (see plate 54), its embellishment with mosaics of glorious colours, and the great inventiveness and symbolism of the detail. The traditional sharp acanthus foliage of the Greeks was united with the emblems of Christianity, such as the circle, the cross, the vine, and the dove: the peacock also is frequently seen. Figure sculpture was rarely used, but groups of figures were used in great profusion in the gold-ground mosaics that covered the upper part of the walls and the vaults and domes of the magnificent Byzantine buildings. The churches of Ravenna, in Italy, have somewhat similar characteristics: S. Vitale, A.D. 535, the basilica churches of S. Apollinare Nuovo, A.D. 493-525, S. Apollinare in Classe, A.D. 535-45, together with the Baptisteries, are rich in mosaics and sculptured capitals of the 6th and 7th centuries. In the cathedrals of Torcello, A.D. 670, and Murano, and the beautiful S. Mark's at Venice, marbles and mosaics were used in great profusion to enhance the architecture. The sketch plans given on plate 53 are typical of Byzantine planning, in which the symbolism of the circle and cross are used as constructive features. This symbolism is a marked feature in Byzantine ornament; interlacing circles and crosses mingle with the acanthus or the vine, and are cut with a peculiar V-shaped section. The circular drill is largely used at the sinking of the leaves, and but little of the background is visible in the sculptured ornament of this period.

Pierced marble screens of interlaced foliage, or the fret in combination with the circle, were frequently used (see plate 53). A large number of pierced parapets in S. Mark's are carved in low relief, with various modifications of the interlacing Guilloche, or circles.

FRIEZE FROM THE CHURCH OF SAINT-GILLES. PROVENCE.

PORTION OF ENGLISH MS.
A D 1020. BRITISH MUSEUM.

DETAIL FROM DOORWAY.
S⸍ AGOSTINA.

CAPITAL
FROM
LAON

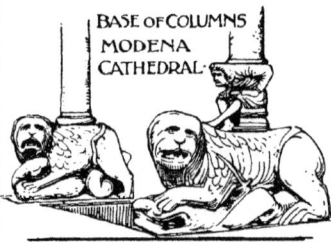

BASE of COLUMNS
MODENA
CATHEDRAL.

PORTAL
FROM
SAINT-
-GILLES.
PROVENCE

BASE OF COLUMNS. WEST
DOOR VERONA CATHEDRAL

32

ROMANESQUE ARCHITECTURE & ORNAMENT.

Romanesque architecture differs from Roman chiefly in the universal use of the arch, the absence of the classic entablature, and in the imagery and symbolism of its sculpture and ornament, doubtless due to Northern influence. One of the earliest existing buildings of this style is the church of S. Ambrogio, Milan (11th century), which has a nave and aisles, three eastern apses, and a western atrium, surrounded by an open arcade, enriched with vigorous reliefs of interlaced ornament and animals. Contemporary in date is S. Michele, Pavia, with a nave and transepts and central cupola: there is a single eastern apse, having an open external gallery and bands of sculptured ornament. This and the frequent use of the lion or griffin as a support for pillars, are characteristic of the Lombardic style, and are seen at S. Michele, Lucca, and the Cathedral, Baptistry, and the Campanile of Pisa.

It was, however, in France and Germany that the Romanesque reached its highest development, principally in the south and southwest of France, where the churches are distinguished for the richness of the west fronts.

S. Trophime, Arles (12th century), has a fine low semi-circular projecting porch, resting upon a sculptured frieze and pillars. A cloister, with arcading of coupled columns richly sculptured, is attached to this church; while S. Gilles (1076) has a low projecting porch of three arches, enriched with vigorous sculpture and ornament (plate 12).

The Cathedral at Angoulême has a vaulted nave, with three cupolas, and a west front with recessed arcading and figures: two square towers, with open arcading and conical spires, rise from the angles of the façade. Notre Dame, Poitiers, is even more rich in its gabled west front, having a fine doorway with two tiers of arcading above. The façade is flanked by two circular turrets, with massive columns attached, having an open arcade above, with a conical spire; enriched corbel tables are carried across the front, over the door, the upper arcade and window, and round the turrets.

Saint-Front, Périgueux, has a richly sculptured west front and nave of the 11th century, to which was added in 1150 a larger church similar in plan to S. Mark's at Venice (a Greek cross, see plate 54), and roofed with five cupolas in stone. In central France there was the magnificent Abbey Church of Cluny, with its range of six towers; and in Germany this number of towers is found at the great Romanesque churches of Speyer, Worms, and Laach, with their singular western apse and external clearstory gallery.

Plate 12 illustrates a few of the chief features of Romanesque ornament. The upper frieze is similar to the Roman scroll, but less vigorous in modelling, and with a rounder form of serration of leaf form. The Laon capital has rich interlacing ornament and animals that suggest Scandinavian influence. The portal of Saint-Gilles shows the exuberant carving and storiation that characterized many of the churches of south-west France.

A CELTIC INITIAL
1

2 INITIAL
FROM THE GOSPELS OF
LINDISFARNE
END OF 7TH CENTURY.
BRITISH MUSEUM.

CELTIC INTERLACEING FRET
3

4 INTERLACED ANIMALS. FROM THE BOOK
OF KELLS. 8TH CENTY. BRITISH MUSEUM

5

CAREW CROSS.

6 BRONZE
SHIELD ENRICHED WITH RED
ENAMELS. BRITISH MUSEUM.

7 PORTION OF THE
TRUMPET PATTERN.
OR DIVERGENT
SPIRAL. FROM
THE BOOK OF
DURROW. TRINITY COLLEGE, DUBLIN.

CELTIC ORNAMENT.

No period in the history of art is more remarkable than the Celtic. The carved stone architecture and crosses, the bronzes, enamels, and silversmith's work, the splendid illuminated books and manuscripts with capitals and borders, full of imagery and intricacy of detail, and the clear and accurate writing of the text are all indications of the culture and love of ornament of the early Irish people, showing a remarkable preference for the spiral and interlacing forms. The bronze shield (fig. 6), with its spirals and bosses of enamel enriched with the northern " Fylfot " is a typical example of the 2nd or 3rd century, A.D. Then comes the trumpet pattern or divergent spiral, which, seen in its infancy on the bronze shield, reached a great degree of elaboration in the 8th and 9th centuries, A.D. (figs. 2 to 7), being typical of Celtic work up to the middle of the 11th century when all trace of this spiral is lost. The interlacing bird and animal forms used from the 8th to the 14th centuries are doubtless derived from Byzantine and Lombardic sources. The serpent or dragon, which is such a marked feature from the 7th to the 15th century must have been borrowed from the north, as Ireland had no traditions of snakes or dragons, and it is to Scandinavia, with its legend of Fafni, that we must look for the origin of the dracontine treatment. It is this Zormorpic character that distinguishes the Celtic from all other styles of ornament except Scandinavian. The obverse of the magnificent processional Cross of Cong (A.D. 1123), is divided into 46 panels of decorations, and convoluted snakes occupy 38 of them.

The illustrations given here from the Lismore crosier are typical examples of this Celtic dracontine treatment. The early or Pagan period is noted for its bronze work, cast and wrought, and enriched with Champleve enamels. The fine chalice of Ardagh (page 116) and the Tara Brooch (plate 40) 7th century, are splendid examples of the Christian period dating from St. Patrick, A.D. 440-460. The beautiful Book of Kells, the Book of Armagh, the Book of Durrow, manuscripts of the early part of the 9th century (Trinity College, Dublin), and the Book of Durham, called the Lindisfarne Gospels, A.D. 689-721, written by Eadfrith, and illuminated by Ethelwald, are a tribute to the vitality, assimilation of ideas, and the culture and wonderful craftmanship of the early Irish people. In Irish manuscripts gold is not used, except in the Lindisfarne Gospels, where a minute quantity is used.

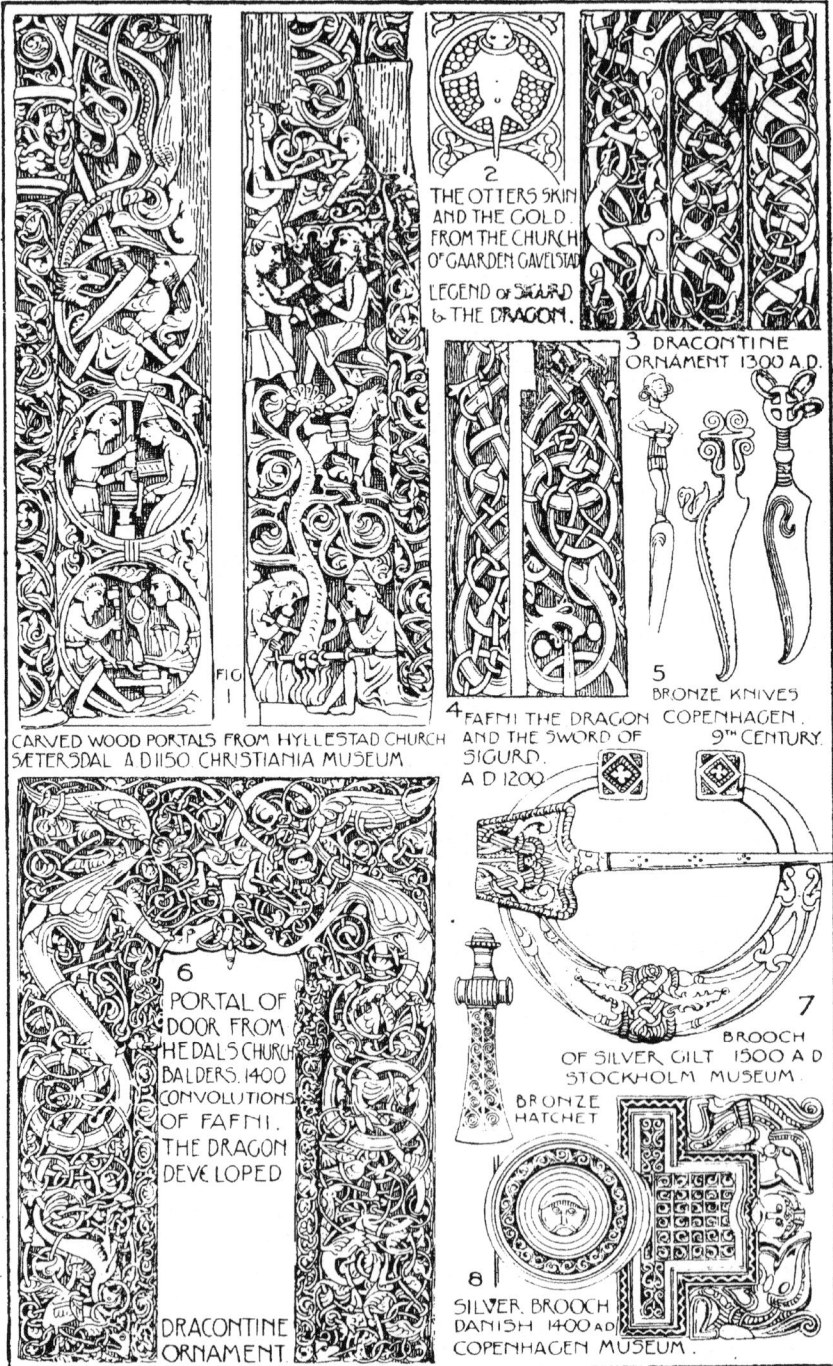

FIG I

CARVED WOOD PORTALS FROM HYLLESTAD CHURCH
SÆTERSDAL A D 1150 CHRISTIANIA MUSEUM

2 THE OTTERS SKIN AND THE GOLD FROM THE CHURCH Of GAARDEN GAVELSTAD

LEGEND of SIGURD & THE DRAGON.

3 DRACONTINE ORNAMENT 1300 A.D.

4 FAFNI THE DRAGON AND THE SWORD OF SIGURD. A D 1200

5 BRONZE KNIVES COPENHAGEN. 9TH CENTURY.

6 PORTAL OF DOOR FROM HEDALS CHURCH BALDERS. 1400 CONVOLUTIONS OF FAFNI. THE DRAGON DEVELOPED

DRACONTINE ORNAMENT

7 BROOCH OF SILVER GILT 1500 A D STOCKHOLM MUSEUM.

BRONZE HATCHET

8 SILVER BROOCH DANISH 1400 A D COPENHAGEN MUSEUM

SCANDINAVIAN ORNAMENT.

The beautiful bronze and silver jewellery and implements of war of the early Viking period, found in Norway, Sweden, and Denmark, display no trace of plant forms in their ornamentation, the latter consisting wholly of interlacing animal forms—chiefly the dragon. The Viking ship found at Sandifiord in 1880, although destitute of ornament, shows traces of the " Bronze Dragon Prow," referred to in the early Scandinavian Sagas. At the commencement of the 12th century, plant forms are found mingled with the dragons, and figure sculpture became important in treating of the myths of the gods; Frey, Woden, Thor, and Tyr, of the pagan period, being influenced by the newer cult in religion. This is shown by the Sigurd Overlap.

The farmer Hreithmar had three sons—Otter, Fafni, and Regin the smith; and three of the Scandinavian gods—Woden, Hœni, and Loki—wandered towards the farm, and, through misunderstanding, Loki killed Otter. For this the three gods were seized, and released only on payment of enough gold to cover the skin of Otter (fig. 2) when hung up by the nose. This price was procured by Loki, who compelled the dwarf Andwari to surrender all the gold he possessed, as well as a magic ring, which carried with it a curse that for eight lives the gold should be fatal to its owner. Then Hreithmar was slain by his surviving sons for the treasure, which was carried off to a great mound on Gnita Heath by Fafni, who lay round his plunder in the form of a dragon. Regin, his brother, in order to obtain the treasure, prompted Sigurd, his foster son, to slay the dragon. Sigurd, in testing his sword, broke it in twain; thereupon Regin made him a magic sword, with which he lay in the trail of the dragon, and pierced it through (figs. 1-4). Then Regin took out the heart of the dragon, which Sigurd cut into pieces and toasted while Regin slept. Sigurd, burning his fingers, placed them in his mouth, and tasted the blood of Fafni, the dragon (fig. 1), and, lo! he heard the voice of birds saying that Regin was plotting to kill him. Then Sigurd killed Regin, ate the heart of Fafni, placed the treasure on the back of the noble horse Grani, and departed, only to be slain for the gold by Gunnar, who for this crime was cast into the pit of serpents (fig. 1).[1]

This myth explains much of the Scandinavian ornament, for in figs. 1 and 2 the story is told in a series of incidents remarkable for the fertility of invention and dracontine ornamentation. Halton Cross, in Lancashire, and a slab at Kirk Andreas, Isle of Man, illustrate the same subjects, dating from the 11th century. In later times, the dragon becomes more pronounced in character, until in the 14th century it fills the whole portal with the beautiful interlacing ornament (fig. 6).

" The Pagan-Christian Overlap in the North," by H. Colley March, M.D. (Lond.).

NORMAN & GOTHIC ARCHITECTURE.

English Gothic architecture has been broadly divided into periods for the purpose of classifying the styles, the following being the most generally accepted :—

By Sharpe.[1]		A.D.		By Rickman.[2]			A.D.
Roman-esque	Saxon	1066		Norman	-	-	1066-1189
	Norman	1066-1145		Early English	-	-	1189-1307
Gothic	Transitional	1145-1190		Decorated	-	-	1307-1379
	Lancet	1190-1245		Perpendicular	-	-	1379-1483
	Curvilinear	1245-1360		Tudor	-	-	1483-1546
	Rectilinear	1360-1550					

Most of our magnificent cathedrals were founded, A.D. 1066-1170, by Norman bishops, some upon the old Saxon foundations, such as Canterbury and York, or near the original Saxon buildings, as at Winchester, or upon new sites, such as Norwich and Peterborough; and were without exception more magnificent erections than those of the anterior period, portions of the older style still existing in many cathedrals, showing the fusion of Roman and Byzantine architecture with the more personal and vigorous art of the Celtic, Saxon, and Scandinavian peoples.

Lincoln is a typical English plan, showing no trace of the semi-circular apsidal arrangement so universal in Norman and French cathedrals. Each vertical division in the nave, the choir, and transept is termed a bay. On plate 15 is an illustration of four typical bays of English cathedrals, showing the development of style from the 12th to the 15th century. The general characteristic of each bay is given separately, but obviously it can only be approximate, as the building of each cathedral was influenced by local considerations, each period necessarily overlapping its predecessor, thus forming a transitional style. For instance, in the choir of Ripon Cathedral the aisle and clearstory have semi-circular Norman windows, and the nave arcading has pointed arches. In the triforium and clearstory arcading, round arches are seen side by side with the pointed arch.

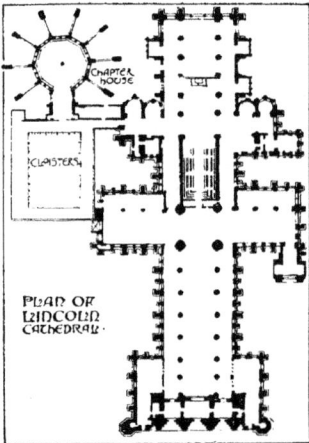

PLAN OF LINCOLN CATHEDRAL.

The PIERS—sometimes termed columns—of these bays have

1 "The Seven Periods of Church Architecture," by Edmund Sharpe.
2 "Gothic Architecture," by Thomas Rickman.

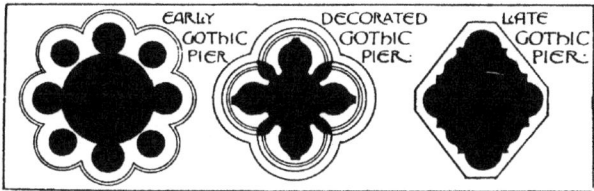

distinctive features which are characteristic of each period of the Gothic development.

Sketch plans are here given showing the changes that took place in the section of the pier from 1066 to 1500. The same general characteristics are observed in the arch mouldings and string courses.

CHARACTERISTICS OF THE NORMAN PERIOD.

NAVE ARCADING.—The universal use of the round arch, cylindrical or rectangular piers, with semi-circular shafts attached to each face. Capitals cubical and cushion-shaped. Arch mouldings enriched with concentric rows of Chevron and Billet ornament.

TRIFORIUM.—In early work, of one arch. In later work, two or four small arches carried on single shafts under one large semi-circular arch.

CLEARSTORY.—One window, with an open arcading in front, of three arches, the centre one larger and often stilted. This arcade forms a narrow gallery in the thickness of the Clearstory wall. The roof of the nave of wood, flat and panelled, roof of the aisles semi-circular quadripartite vaulting. An arcading of semi-circular arches was usually placed upon the wall, under the aisle windows. Early windows are narrow, flush with the external wall, and deeply splayed on the inside. Later windows are recessed externally, with jamb-shafts and capitals supporting an enriched moulded arch. A few semi-circular rose windows still remain, of which a fine example is to be found in Barfrestone Church, Kent.

RIEVAULX ABBEY.
The EAST WALL.
LANCET PERIOD.

39

EARLY ENGLISH OR LANCET PERIOD.

The Lancet or pointed arch universal.

CAPITALS, of three lobed foliage and circular abacus. The pier arch mouldings, alternate rounds and hollows deeply cut and enriched with the characteristic dog's tooth ornament. A hood moulding which terminates in bosses of foliage or sculptured heads invariably surrounds the arch mouldings. This moulded hood when used externally is termed a " Dripstone," and when used horizontally over a square headed window, a " Label."

The TRIFORIUM has a single or double arch, which covers the smaller or subordinate arches, the spandrels being enriched with a sunk or pierced trefoil or quatrefoil. The Triforium piers are solid, having delicate shafts attached to them, carrying arch mouldings of three orders, and enriched with the dog's tooth ornament or trefoil foliage.

The CLEARSTORY lancet windows are in triplets, with an arcading on the inner face of the wall. The vaulting shaft occasionally springs from the floor, but more usually from a corbel above the nave capitals, and finishes under the clearstory string with an enriched capital, from which springs the simple vaulting usually quadripartite or hexapartite in form. Early windows in small churches were arranged in couplets, and at the east end, usually in triplets, with grisaille stained glass. The example given on the previous page from the east end of Rievaulx Abbey shows a finely proportioned window and its arrangement. Figure sculpture, beautiful and refined in treatment, was frequently used upon external walls.

The figures of Saints and Bishops were placed singly under triangular pediments and cusped arches, of which there are fine examples at Wells, Lichfield, Exeter, and Salisbury (fig. 5, plate 18). Splendid examples of circular rose windows are to be seen in the north and south transepts of Lincoln Cathedral, also at York, but they are comparatively rare in England, while France possesses over 100 of the finest and most important examples of this type. They are to be seen in the Cathedrals of Notre Dame, Rouen, Chartres, and Rheims.

DECORATED OR GEOMETRIC PERIOD.

In this, the piers have engaged shafts, with capitals having plain mouldings, or enriched with finely carved foliage of the oak, maple, or mallow, seen in perfection at Southwell Minster, which contains the finest carving of this period—1280-1315 (plate 18). The pier arches have mouldings of three orders, also enriched, usually with the characteristic ball, flower, or foliage, similar to that upon the capitals.

The TRIFORIUM consists of double arches, with subordinate cusped arches adorned with Geometric tracery. The inner arcading of the Clearstory is absent, the one large window being divided by mullions

40

PETERBOROUGH · LINCOLN · LICHFIELD · WINCHESTER

CLEAR-STORY

TRIFORIUM

AISLE WINDOW

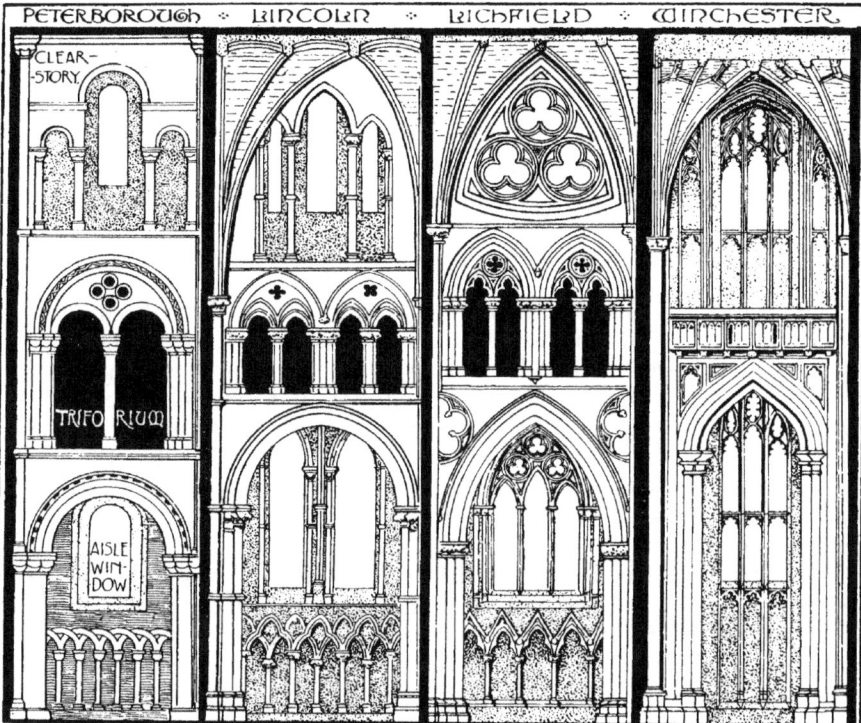

1 NORMAN 2 LANCET 3 GEOMETRIC 4 PERPENDICULAR
FOUR BAYS OF TYPICAL ENGLISH CATHEDRALS 12TH TO THE 15TH CENTURY

EARLY GOTHIC SCULPTURE & ARCADING SALISBURY CATHEDRAL EXTERIOR
5

6 LATE DECORATED WINDOW BEVERLEY

7 EARLY GOTHIC. WEST-MINSTER

8

PERPENDICULAR WINDOW WEST MINSTER

and geometrical tracery, or by equilateral triangles enriched with circular and bar tracery (fig. 3, plate 15). Above the pier capitals an enriched corbel is usually placed from which springs the vaulting shafts, terminating with a richly carved capital under the Clearstory string. The aisle arcading, as a rule, is very beautiful, having geometric tracery and finely proportioned mouldings, the aisle windows with mullions and bold geometric tracery. The circular rose windows of the transepts are typical of this period.

PERPENDICULAR AND TUDOR.

The PIERS of this style are lofty and enriched with shallow mouldings carried round the pier arch, where capitals are introduced. They frequently resemble a band round the pier at the springing of the arch, or occasionally they are octagonal in form, and decorated with an angular treatment of the vine. In some instances the upper part of the plain octagonal capital is relieved with an embattlement. The latter is also frequently used as a cresting for the elaborate perpendicular screens, or for relieving the clearstory strings, or on the transoms or the lofty windows.

The TRIFORIUM is absent in this period, the bay consisting of two horizontal divisions only. The CLEARSTORY, owing to the suppression of the Triforium, becomes of more importance. The windows are large and often in pairs, with vertical mullions extending to the arch mouldings of the window head. The aisle windows are similar, and when lofty have horizontal transoms, on which the battlement ornament is displayed. The aisle arcading being also suppressed, all plain wall space was covered with perpendicular surface tracery. Enrichment of this type was used in the greatest profusion upon walls, parapets, buttresses, and arches, also upon the jambs and soffits of doorways. This, together with the use of the four-centred arch, forms the characteristic feature of the Perpendicular or Tudor period.

The remarkable growth of the Gothic style during the 13th and 14th centuries was contemporary in England, France, Flanders, Germany, and in a less degree in Italy. One of the most beautiful churches in Italy is S. Maria della Spina, at Pisa, with its rich · crocketed spires and canopies, features which were repeated a little later at the tomb of the famous *Scaligers* at Verona. Gothic is differentiated by the use of the ogee arch with cusps and pierced quatrefoils.

At Venice there are many magnificent examples of Gothic architecture, remarkable for the beautiful central grouping of the windows, arcades, and balconies and the prevalence of the ogee arch, with cusps and pierced quatrefoils and rich foliated capitals. The façade of the Doge's Palace, with its great colonnade of 36 pillars with rich foliated capitals (see Ruskin's "Seven Lamps of Architecture," plate V.), and the Porta della Carta, or entrance, with its magnificent doorway flanked by figures and canopies and surmounted by a traceried window, and gable enriched with exquisitely carved crockets and finials of foliage and figures, are by Bartolommeno Buon (1420-71), who also built the Foscari Palace. Other examples are the Casa, or Ca d'oro, and the Palazzi Pisani, Conterini Fasan, and Danieli, each with beautiful grouping of windows, pierced quatrefoil, and rich balconies.

It was in France and England that Gothic architecture reached its culmination. The abbeys and cathedrals, with spires and towers enriched with vigorous and beautiful sculpture, arcadings and canopies, with cusps, crockets, and finials, and the splendid traceried windows, filled with glorious stained glass, are all tributes to the religious zeal and splendid craftsmanship of the middle ages.

The west fronts of the larger cathedrals of France have deeply-recessed triple porches, covered with figure sculpture (page 53), magnificent towers with lofty open tracery, as at Amiens and Rheims, and splendid rose windows, as those of Chartres (an early example of plate tracery), Rheims, Amiens, and the Cathedral and S. Ouen at Rouen, the two latter with rich flamboyant tracery.

French cathedrals are invariably of the periapsidal plan, with the semi-circular eastern ambulatory, surrounded by three or five radiating chapels. Aisle chapels also are frequently introduced between the bases of the flying buttresses, giving a greater width across the church. In early cathedrals, the triforium chamber, or upper aisle and its arcade, was similar to English examples; but early in the 13th century the triforium gallery was reduced to the thickness of the nave wall, and the outer arcading glazed. Later, the triforium, with its glazed arcading, became merged into the great clearstory windows, with their wealth and glory of coloured glass.

English cathedrals show a marked contrast in scale to contemporary French buildings. The English nave and choir are less in height and width but greater in length than French cathedrals. For instance, Westminster is the highest of our English cathedrals, with its nave and choir 103 ft. from floor to roof, 30 ft. wide, and 505 ft. in length. York is next with 101 ft. from floor to roof, 45 ft. wide, and 486 ft. in length. Salisbury is 84 ft. from floor to roof, 32 ft. wide, and 450 ft. in length; and Canterbury 80 ft. from floor to roof, 39 ft. wide, and 514 ft. in length. Lincoln with 82 ft. and Peterborough with 81 ft. are the only other examples reaching 80 ft. in height: York, with 45 ft., being the only one reaching above 40 ft. in width of nave. The measurements of contemporary French cathedrals, on the other hand, being as follows:—Chartres, 106 ft. from floor to roof, 46 ft. wide, and 415 ft. in length; Notre Dame, 112 ft. from floor to roof, 46 ft. wide, and 410 ft. in length; Rheims, 123 ft. from floor to roof, 41 ft. wide, and 485 ft. in length; while that at Beauvais reaches the great height of 153 ft. in the nave, 45 ft. in width, and only 263 ft. in length.

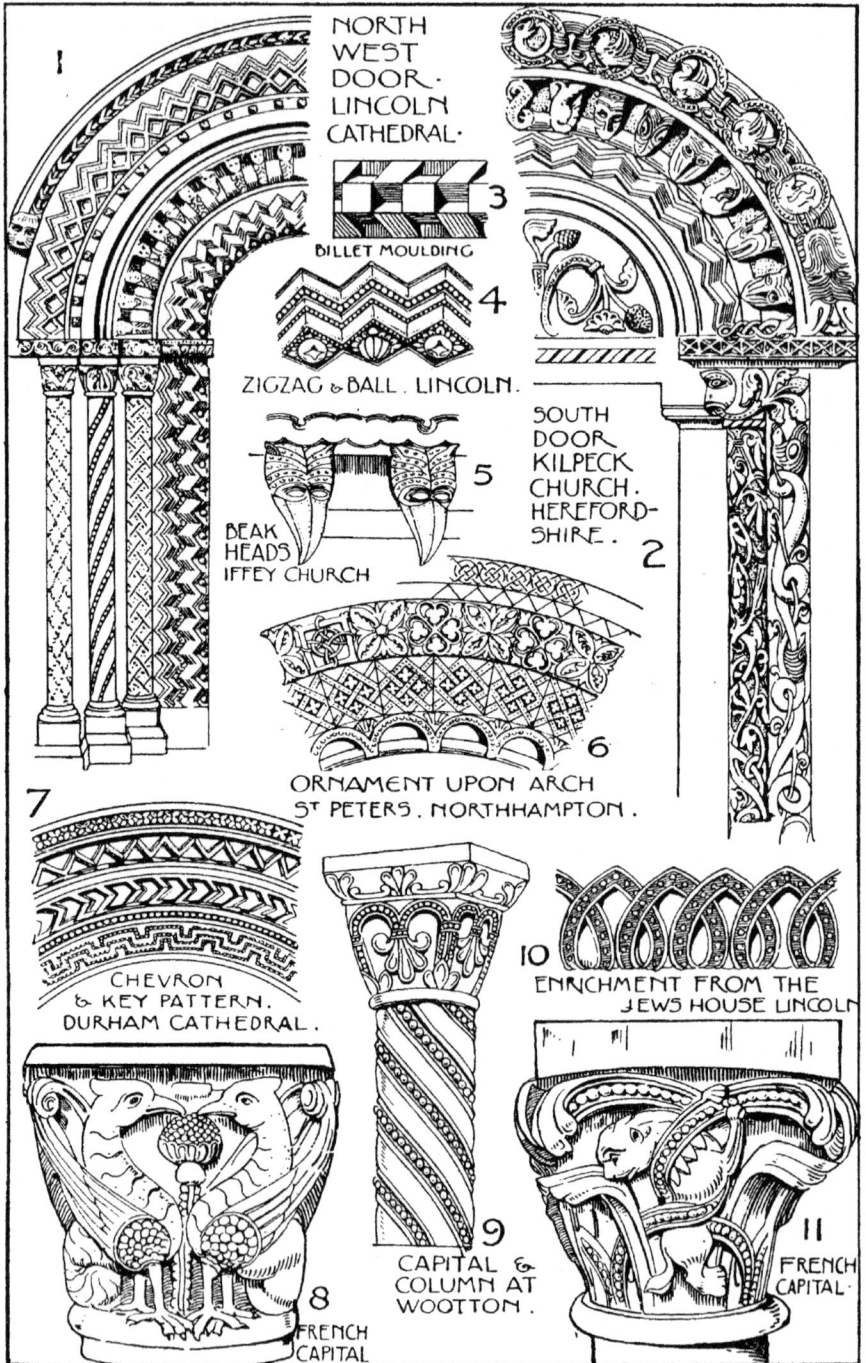

1

NORTH WEST DOOR. LINCOLN CATHEDRAL.

3

BILLET MOULDING

4

ZIGZAG & BALL. LINCOLN.

5

BEAK HEADS IFFEY CHURCH

SOUTH DOOR KILPECK CHURCH. HEREFORD-SHIRE.

2

6

ORNAMENT UPON ARCH ST PETERS. NORTHHAMPTON.

7

CHEVRON & KEY PATTERN. DURHAM CATHEDRAL.

10

ENRICHMENT FROM THE JEWS HOUSE LINCOLN

9

CAPITAL & COLUMN AT WOOTTON.

8

FRENCH CAPITAL

11

FRENCH CAPITAL

NORMAN ORNAMENT.

Norman Architecture was distinguished by the use of the traditional semi-circular arch, superseded by the pointed arch of the early Gothic period. These semi-circular arches in the earlier dates were decorated with rudely executed carvings, cut or worked with the axe. Later Norman work is very rich, the mouldings being well carved with enrichments of the Chevron, the Cable, Pallet, Star, Fret or Key Patterns ; the lozenge and the beading or pearling. Characteristic features of this period also are the beakhead (fig. 5), and the corbel-table, which was a series of heads of men or animals, from which spring small arches supporting the parapet. Many rich examples of Norman surface ornament are still extant ; at Christchurch, Hants, a beautiful intersecting arcading of semi-circular arches occurs, the enrichment above being a scale or imbricated pattern ; at St. Peter's, Northampton, a very rich example of surface ornamentation may be seen (fig. 6).

Floral forms are but rarely used in Norman ornament ; instances are known of the use of the rose and the fir-apple, but they are the exception and not the rule.

Early doorways usually have a square head recessed under semi-circular arch mouldings, decorated with the Chevron, Key, or Beakhead. The semi-circular Tympanum over the door was plain or enriched with rude sculpture in low relief. Later doors show a great profusion of ornament in the archivolt and arch mouldings, which are often carried down the jamb mouldings. The recessed columns are also enriched with the Chevron, or diagonal lines of pearling (fig. 1), and have sculptured capitals showing a classical tendency in the arrangement of acanthus foliage and the volute. Fine examples of this period may be seen in the west front of Lincoln Cathedral (fig. 1), the Galilee porch at Durham, and the west door of Iffley Church, Oxfordshire. A fine, deeply recessed semi-circular Norman doorway is at Tutbury Church, having a richly recessed window over, now filled with flamboyant tracery.

Early Norman Capitals are usually cubical or cushion-shaped, with a square or cruciform abacus, or occasionally octagonal as at Durham, or circular as at Gloucester, and enriched with the Chevron, Star, or Anthemion. The capitals being escalloped with segments of circles, or enriched with Volutes or the Anthemion. Early examples are in the White Tower, and St. Bartholomew, London. Later Capitals, usually rich in ornamentation, are found at St. Peter's, Northampton and Wooton, or more frequently that have interlacing bands of ornament and animals ; others with figures or " Storied Capitals," as in the North Porch, Wells.

In the transition period—end of 12th century—Capitals were concave or bell-shaped, with foliage of the serrated water-leaf type clinging to the bell and turning up under the abacus, forming a Volute. This foliage was varied in type and vigorous in technique. Fine examples are at Christ Church, Oxford, and at Canterbury Cathedral.

2

STONE BOSS

1

STONE: SPANDRIL FROM CHANCEL ARCADE ♦ STONE CHURCH. KENT.

4 CROCKET YORK CATHEDRAL

3
EARLY GOTHIC GLASS · SALISBURY

5 FROM SALISBURY CATHEDRAL

6
FROM ELY CATHEDRAL

8
TOOTH ORNAMENT

9 PETERBOROUGH

DIAPER WESTMINSTER

ELY CATHEDRAL

10
EARLY ENGLISH CLUSTERED CAPITAL.

LINCOLN CATHEDRAL

11
EARLY FRENCH GOTHIC. NOTRE DAME.

12
EARLY FRENCH CAPITAL. RHEIMS CATHEDRAL

ARLY GOTHIC.

The NORMAN style was succeeded by the pointed, or GOTHIC style, remarkable for its variety, its beauty of proportion, and the singular grace and vigour of its ornament. Showing no traditions, beyond Sicilian and Arabian influence, it grew rapidly, and reached a high degree of perfection in France and England. The massive and barbaric character of the Norman style gave place to the light clustered shafts and well-proportioned mouldings of the early English Gothic, with its capitals characterised by a circular abacus, and the typical three-lobed foliage growing upwards from the necking of the shafts, thence spreading out in beautiful curves and spirals under the abacus. This tendency to the spiral line is peculiar to the early Gothic, and differentiates it from the Decorated and Perpendicular Period. The diagrams of the three crockets here given show the distinctive character of English Gothic ornament.

Early Gothic, three-lobed leaves arranged in spiral lines. Decorated Gothic, with natural types of foliage, such as the oak and maple, with a flowing indulating line. Perpendicular Gothic, showing the vine and leaves as elements, and arranged in a square and angular manner. The same features and characteristics are observed in the borders here given. The beautiful carved spandril from the Chancel Arcade, Stone Church, Kent (fig. 1), is one of the most beautiful examples of English ornament, remarkable for the vigour and flexibility of curve, its recurring forms of ornamentation, and admirable spacing, typical of much of our early English foliage from about 1170-1280.

The type of foliage in early English stained glass is somewhat similar to contemporary carved work, but showing more of the profile of the leaf, and it has a geometric or radiating arrangement in addition to the spiral forms of foliage (plate 39), and the admirable spacing of the ornament shows the skill in design that the mediæval craftsman possessed.

CAPITALS FROM CHAPTER HOUSE, SOUTHWELL.

FROM THE TRIFORIUM OF NAVE. St ALBANS.

A MISERERE.

PARAPET, BEVERLEY MINSTER.

THE BALL-FLOWER.

ALTERNATE BALL-FLOWER.

FOUR-LEAVED-FLOWER.

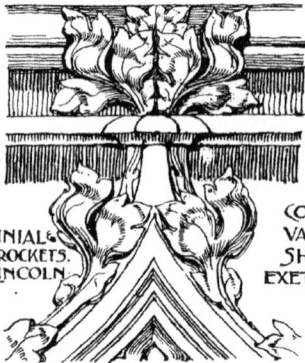

FINIAL & CROCKETS. LINCOLN.

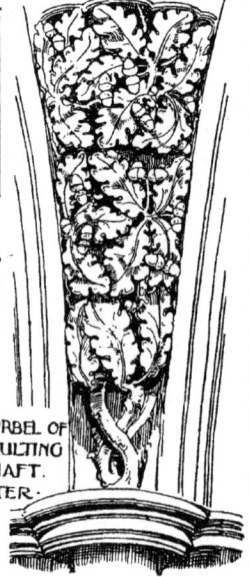

CORBEL OF VAULTING SHAFT. EXETER.

DECORATED OR GEOMETRIC GOTHIC.

Decorated Gothic is remarkable for its geometric tracery, its natural types of foliage, and the undulating character of line and form, in its ornamental details. The foliage of the oak, the vine, the maple, the rose, and the ivy were introduced in much luxuriance and profusion, being carved with great delicacy and accuracy. Lacking the dignity and architectonic qualities of the early Gothic foliage, it surpassed it in brilliancy and inventiveness of detail. The capitals, enriched with adaptations from nature, carved with admirable precision, were simply attached round the bell, giving variety and charm of modelling, but lacking that unity which was so characteristic of early work.

FINIAL & CROCKETS. EXETER CATHEDRAL.

The illustrations from Southwell are characteristic examples of the richly-carved clustered capitals of this period. The arch mouldings were also enriched with foliage of a similar type, and at the springing of the vaulting shaft of the nave, beautiful carved corbels, such as those at Exeter, were used, while the walls, screens, and parapets, were diapered with low relief carving.

Crockets and finials, which were introduced in the early Gothic period, were now treated with exceeding richness and used in the greatest profusion. A characteristic example is given here from Exeter Cathedral.

The Queen Eleanor crosses (erected 1291-4), are perhaps the richest examples of the decorated period, showing the exuberance of modelling and the versatility and skill of the English craftsman in the finest period of Naturalistic foliage (1280-1315).

The "Ball Flower" so characteristic of the decorated period, replaced the equally characteristic "Tooth Ornament" of the preceding style, and was much used in some buildings, even to excess—as in the south aisle of Gloucester Cathedral. It is found in the hollows round doorways, win-

WALL DIAPER. WESTMINSTER.

dows, arches, and canopies, and it frequently alternates with the "Four-petalled Flower."

CORNICE FROM BISHOP BECKINGTON'S SHRINE WELLS CATHEDRAL

1

3 2

TUDOR FLOWER WESTMINSTER

FROM UFFORD CHURCH. SUFFOLK

quod facru tau

4 5

FRIEZE FROM ROOD SCREEN
TRUNCH CHURCH NORFOLK

TRUNCH CHURCH. NORFOLK.

6

FROM ROOD-SCREEN
SOUTH POOL CHURCH.
DEVON

SCREEN TO
LADY CHAPEL
MANCHESTER
CATHEDRAL
9

7 UPPER PART OF SOUTH PORCH. LAVENHAM CHURCH. SUFFOLK

8 FIREPLACE IN TATTERSHALL CASTLE
LINCOLNSHIRE 1433-55

PERPENDICULAR GOTHIC.

Late or rectilinear Gothic is characterized by a rigidity of line in construction and ornament. The one exception is the beautiful fan-vaulting, such as that in the cloisters at Gloucester Cathedral, and in Henry VIII. Chapel at Westminster, which are not approached by any Continental example for beauty of craftsmanship or the scientific precision of their masonry. The many splendid towers, having elaborate panelled tracery, and capped with pinnacles, open parapets, and battlements, such as those at Wrexham and S. Mary's, Taunton, are also characteristic of this period. The windows, with vertical mullions running to the window-head, which is frequently a four-centred arch, have one or more transoms, enriched with battlements or Tudor flowers, to divide the lofty windows horizontally (plate 15). The many choir screens and stalls, with their canopies, have panels, friezes, crestings, and finials, and are frequently carved with an angular treatment of the vine and its tendrils, more or less conventionalized (figs. 1-7), the Tudor flower being perhaps the most prevalent. The freedom and flexibility of the modelling and carving of the middle period of Gothic, was replaced by a stiff symmetrical arrangement of foliage, and the painted diapers succeeded the carved ones of the earlier period. The terminals of the ends of pews were frequently enriched with foliated " Poppy-heads," often of great beauty.

Heraldic forms, such as shields, with their supporters, together with badges and crests, were largely associated with the ornament in the richer buildings of this period, such as King's College Chapel at Cambridge, and Henry VIII.'s Chapel at Westminster.

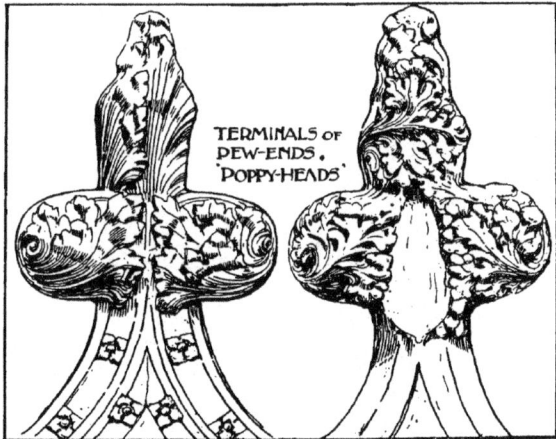

TERMINALS of PEW-ENDS. POPPY-HEADS

The piers of the nave are usually rectangular or lozenge in section, consisting of a few rounds and double ogee moulds, which are frequently carried round the arch without the intervening capital; or an octagonal capital, with the typical square foliated ornament, is carried by some of the round members of the pier; or a series of moulded capitals, without enrichment, is employed. The only enrichment in the hollows of the strings and arch-mouldings is a four-petalled flower, alternate square and circular (figs. 7 and 8).

EARLY GOTHIC STONE CARVING. NOTRE DAME. PARIS.

1

WOOD CARVING

CANOPY OF
STALLS IN
CATHEDRAL,
AMIENS
LATE GOTHIC.

2

3
13ᵀᴴ CENTURY CAPITAL

4
14ᵀᴴ CENTURY CARVINGS.

5

FRENCH GOTHIC.

French cathedrals show a marked contrast in scale and enrichment to those of England, being wider, shorter, and higher in proportion, and the sculpture bolder, more profuse, and larger in scale than in contemporary English cathedrals. The principal doorways are also on a large scale, and are usually enriched with numerous statues, placed under canopies, which cover the whole of the recessed arch; whilst the central pier of the door, carrying the figure of the Madonna or a bishop, supports the tympanum (the space within the arch), which is also covered with horizontal bands of sculpture. The figure sculpture of the late 13th and early 14th centuries has considerable skill of composition, and well-arranged draperies; broad and simple in mass, and vigorous in execution.

The gables of the doors are frequently enriched with crockets and finials, or with beautiful open tracery —as in the west doors of Rouen Cathedral. The Cathedral of Amiens has a delightful series of sculptured reliefs of Biblical subjects, called the Bible of Amiens, enclosed within quatre-foil panels, which extends across the lower part of the façade.

The early relief ornament of the 13th century is remarkable for its vigorous carving and boldness of relief. It differs from contemporary English work in having a rounder form of leaf, divided into lobes, with strongly-marked radiating mid-ribs (compare fig. 1, plate 20, with fig. 1, plate 17). The capitals, with the foliage clinging closely to the bell (fig. 3), have not the spiral tendency that characterized English ornament of the same period. The abacus is generally square (page 153), and the clustered pillars and the bell-shaped moulded capitals, without foliage, which are typical of English work, are almost unknown in France. In the 14th century, the foliage, like contemporary carving in England, is naturalistic (figs. 4 and 5, plate 20, and page 157), with a ribbed tool-mark following the direction of the leaf.

Among the many splendid examples of the 15th century, or flamboyant period, are the stalls of Amiens (fig. 2), where flowing tracery is intermingled with rich cusped-arches, open gables, and crocketed pinnacles.

SOUTH DOOR. AMIENS CATHEDRAL

A PORTION OF THE ARCHITRAVE FROM THE BRONZE GATES OF THE BAPTISTERY FLORENCE.
BY LORENZO GHIBERTI. 1425-52. QUATTROCENTO PERIOD.

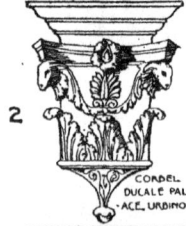

8 INCHES

2

CORBEL
DUCALE PAL
ACE, URBINO

3

4

DRAWING FOR A FRIEZE BY GIOLAMO CURTI 16th Century
IN THE UFFIZI GALLERY FLORENCE Bistar drawing

5

PAGE FROM THE BOOK OF HOURS, OF
BONA SFORZA, DUCHESS OF MILAN
1477-90 BRITISH MUSEUM.

4½ INCHES

6

10 INCHES

MARBLE
TABERNACLE
OR SHRINE
BY ANDREA
FERRUCCI
1528

7

ORNAMENT FROM THE BERNARDO MONUMENT
IN THE CHURCH OF SANTA MARIA DE'FRARI,
VENICE. 1540.

BORDER FROM THE
GRENVILLE SFORZIADA,
1490. BRITISH MUSEUM

FROM THE CHURCH OF SAN GIROLAMO AT FIESOLE

8

ENAMELLED TERRA-COTTA OR DELLA ROBBIA WARE
BY LUCA DELLA ROBBIA, 1450
IN THE CHURCH OF S ONOFRIO ROME

9

PAINTED ORNAMENT FROM THE DUCAL PALACE MANTUA
BY GIOVANNI DA UDINE AND JULIO ROMANO
1530

RENASCENCE ARCHITECTURE & ORNAMENT.

Lombardy, in the north of Italy, had witnessed a singular blending of the old classic art with the vigorous traditions and myths of the Longobards, and the symbolisms of the old Byzantine; thus producing the architecture known as Lombardic, with its multiplicity of small columns and arches, quaint imagery of sculpture, and the frequent use of a lion or dragon as a support for the columns. These are features of the early art at Lucca, and at Bergamo, Padua, Verona, and other towns in Lombardy (see Romanesque, page 33); a beautiful illustration from Lucca is given in the appendix to Ruskin's " Stones of Venice," Vol. I. Contemporary with this period came the Gothic influence with its clustered columns, pointed arches, its cusps and crockets, and its strong vitality, impressing the arts and architecture with a lasting influence; hence, during the 12th and 13th centuries in Italy, this intermingling of styles, traditions, religious beliefs and myths, produced an art barbaric and vigorous in character, the imagery full of suggestiveness, and the detail rich and varied in conception. Yet it was but the herald of a style which culminated in the glorious epoch of the Renascence, a style where symmetry was to play an important part, as in classic art, where refinement of line and detail, of culture and craftsmanship, are found ; and which, though beautiful in proportion, unity of parts, and perfect adaptability, yet lacked that symbolism, suggestiveness, inventiveness and rugged strength of the early Byzantine, Lombardic, and Gothic styles.

Italian Renascence is broadly divided into three periods, viz. :— The tre-cento, or transitional, A.D. 1300-1400 ; the quattro-cento, 1400-1500 ; and the cinque-cento, 1500-1600.

In the tre-cento period the sculpture and decorative arts are marked by dignity of conception, and a mingling of Gothic and classic traditions. One of the earliest examples is the hexagonal pulpit in the Baptistery at Pisa, and in the Cathedral at Siena, by Nicolo Pisano (1206-76), where sculptured panels distinctly classic in treatment, are associated with cusped Gothic arches. Nicolo also executed the beautiful octagonal fountain at Perugia, and was assisted in much of his work by his son Giovanni Pisano, who also executed the pulpit in the Cathedral at Pisa.

A fine monumental work of this period having similar characteristics, is the tomb of S. Peter the Martyr, in the Church of S. Eustovgio, at Milan, by Balducco di Pisa (1308-47).

In the architecture of this period, Gothic forms prevail, together with the use of panelling of white and grey marble, lofty pilasters, pinnacles and gables, enriched with a geometric patterning of marbles or mosaic, and a frequent use of the slender twisted pillar.

The Cathedral at Florence, with its panelling, pointed arches, and rich tracery, was by Arnolfo di Cambio (died 1300), and Francesco Talenti, who completed the nave, choir, and apses in 1321. Arnolfo and Talenti were also the architects for the Church of Santo Croce (1294-1442), and the Palazzo Vecchio, Florence, (1290), where, in 1434, Michelozzo added the beautiful cortile, and C. Salviati and De Faenza, pupils of Vasari, enriched the circular and octagonal pillars with beautiful stucco ornamentation (fig. 2. plate 22), in 1565.

The beautiful campanile by Giotto (1336), Andrea Pisano, and Francesco Talenti, who introduced the upper Gothic windows, is a noble accessory to the Cathedral of Florence. A charming illustration of one of these windows is given in the "Seven Lamps of Architecture," by John Ruskin.

In 1283 Arnolfo introduced some Prato marble pilasters at the angles of "San Giovanni," the octagonal Florentine Baptistery, an ancient building where many of the great citizens of the Republic received their baptism, and it was here that Dante was baptised in May, 1265.

The last of the tre-cento masters was Andrea Pisano (1270-1345), who made the first bronze gate of "San Giovanni," or the Baptistery of Florence. This gate has 28 quatre-foil panels in relief, and bears the inscription "ANDREAS UGOLINI NINI ME FECIT, A.D. MCCCXXX."

The true Renascence or quattro-cento period is remarkable for the vitality of the arts, and the naturalism and versatility of its craftsmen. Brunelleschi (1377-1446), is the first architect (page 64), and Lorenzo Ghiberti (1381-1465) the ornamentist and sculptor, whose chief works are the two bronze gates for the Florentine Baptistery. The first gate (1403-24), has 28 quatre-foil panels similar to the

MONUMENT TO ILARIA DI CARRETTO,
BY JACOPO DELLA QUERCIA.

one by Andrea Pisano, and the last gate (1425-59), has 10 rectangular panels with incidents from the Old Testament in high relief (plate 43).

The styles or framework of these gates, have a series of single figures in niches with circular medallions between them.

The bronze architrave round each of the Ghiberti gates and the earlier gate by Andrea Pisano, are rich examples of quattro-cento design. The details are natural fruits, flowers and foliage, banded together with ribbons, with the introduction of birds, squirrels, etc. The egg-plant and pomegranate portion (fig. 1) is a familiar example.

Other masters of this period were Jacopo della Quercia (1371-1438), who executed the beautiful monument shown on the previous page, to Ilaria di Carretto, in the Cathedral at Lucca. The recumbent figure of Ilaria is sculptured in white marble with perfect simplicity and beauty; another famous work of Jacopo, was the fountain at Siena.

THE "CANTORIA," OR SINGING GALLERY, BY DONATELLO.

Luca della Robbia (1400-82), executed a beautiful organ gallery in marble for the Cathedral at Florence (1431-40), now in the museum of the Opera del Duomo, Florence, with admirable singing and dancing figures, in relief. Donatello (1386-1466), was remarkable for the singular grace and sincerity of his portraiture, especially of children. The dancing figures in relief on the panels of the singing gallery of the Cathedral of Florence are perfect examples of his art.

This frieze of children is a delightful example of one phase of Donatello's craftsmanship, showing the vitality and exuberance of his conception. The peculiar relief, called "*stacciato*," of the figures,

S. GEORGE, BY DONATELLO.

which shows a series of almost flat surfaces, upon which is carved exquisitely delicate reliefs, contrasted with an abrupt contour giving strongly-marked shadows, is typical of much of Donatello's relief-work. An illustration is also given of the famous S. George, from the Gothic church or oratory of Or San Michele, Florence. This church has niches and canopies on the external walls, each with its statue by great quattro-cento masters. Three statues in marble of S. Peter (1412), S. Mark (1412), and S. George (1415), are by Donatello; three in marble, S. Philip (1408), Four Crowned Martyrs, and S. Eligius (1415), by Nanni di Banco; S. John (1415) and S. Matthew (1422), in bronze, by Ghiberti; Christ and S. Thomas (1483), bronze, by Verrochio; and S. Luke (1601), in bronze, by Giovanni da Bologne.

The Monastery of San Marco is one of the remarkable buildings in Florence. Built in 1437-50 by Michelozzo for Cosimo de Medici, it was enriched with the most beautiful frescoes by Fra Angelico (1387-1455).

Savonarola, the great preacher and reformer, was Prior of San Marco from 1489-98.

The art of the medallist, which had declined since the Roman period, now took its position among the arts of the quattro-cento period, under Vittore Pisano, called Pisanello (1380-1451). The vigour of his modelling

RELIEFS FROM THE SINGING GALLERY, BY DONATELLO, IN THE MUSEUM OF THE OPERA DEL DUOMO, FLORENCE.

10 INCHES

1 RELIEF ORNAMENT IN MARBLE. SCHOOL OF LOMBARDI VENICE. 1500.

2 PORTION OF OCTAGONAL COLUMN, WITH STUCCO ENRICHMENT IN THE COURTYARD OF PALLAZZO VECCHIO

4 MARBLE FONT BY PIETRO LOMBARDO IN THE CHURCH OF SANTA MARIA DE' MIRACOLI, VENICE

5 RELIEF PANEL FROM ST MICHELE, VENICE. SCHOOL OF LOMBARDI 16TH CENTURY.

24½ INCHES

3 MARBLE PANEL IN THE CHURCH OF SANTA MARIA DE' MIRACOLI, VENICE 1500 BY PIETRO LOMBARDO AND HIS SONS, TULLIO AND ANTONIO.

6 EACH 14 INCHES

PORTION OF TERRA COTTA PILASTERS. SOUTH KENSINGTON MUSEUM.

59

and the individuality of his medals of the contemporary princes of Italy, are exceedingly fine. Among other remarkable medallists, were Sperandio of Verona (1423-90), Caradossa of Milan (1480-1545), Vincentine of Vicenza (1468-1546), Benvenuto Cellini of Florence (1500-71), Lione Leoni (1498-1560), Pompeoni Leoni (1530-1610), and Pastorino of Siena (1510-91).

Other names of this period were Desiderio da Settignano (1428-64), his masterpiece being the tomb of Carlo Marzuppini, in the Church of Santa Croce, Florence; Mino da Fiesole (1430-84, see frontispiece); Andrea Verrocchio (1435-88), the author of the fine equestrian statue of Bartolommeo Colleone at Venice (see Bronzes); Matteo Civitali (1435-1501); and the Rossellini, a remarkable family of five brothers, of which the most famous was Antonio Rossellini (1427-79), who executed a charming tomb to Cardinal Jacopo di Portogallo, in the Church of the Nunziata, Florence.

The cinque-cento period was the culmination of the Renascence, when architecture, sculpture, painting, and the decorative arts, were under the magnificent patronage of the popes and princes of Italy. Palaces, churches, and public buildings were completed (see Renascence Architecture, pages 64-67), and embellished with beautiful sculptures and decorations; hung with the most sumptuous fabrics of the Venetian, Florentine, and Genoese looms; decorated with altar paintings and mural decorations by the most renowned of painters; and enriched with the magnificent productions of the gold and silversmiths' art, and the loveliest of intarsia, or inlaid woodwork.

THE CUMÆAN SIBYL BY MICHEL ANGELO

The Sistine chapel, built for Sixtus IV., in 1473, by Baccio Pintelli, is decorated with fresco paintings on the walls by the great cinque-cento masters, Luca Signorelli (1441-1524), Sandro Botticelli (1447-1515), Cosimo Rosselli (1439-1506), Perugino, the master of Raphael (1446-1524), Domenico Ghirlandajo (1449-98), and Michel Angelo (1475-1564), who painted "The Last Judgment," on the end wall, and the famous ceiling, with incidents from the Old Testament, and with the prophets Joel, Ezekiel, Jeremiah, Jonah, Daniel, Isaiah, and Zechariah, and the sibyls Erithræa, Perscia, Lybica, Cumæa, and Delphica. These are splendid examples of decorative painting, where unity and dignity of conception, powerful draughtsmanship, and marvellous execution are shown in a remarkable degree.

The New Sacristy of San Lorenzo, Florence, designed and executed by Michel Angelo, having the magnificent tombs of Lorenzo and

TOMB OF LORENZO DE MEDICI.

Guiliano de Medici, with the reclining figures of Dawn and Twilight, Day and Night, show his remarkable versatility, power, and conception of art.

Contemporary with Michel Angelo was Raphael (1483-1520), who displayed the highest capacity for grace and refinement in painting. His chief decorative works are in the Stanze of the Vatican, a series of four rooms. His first Mural painting here was the "Disputa" (1508), in the Camera della Segnatura, followed by the "Poetry, Philosophy, or School of Athens" and "Jurisprudence," the ceiling being painted with figures and arabesques by Sodoma (Bazzi). The Stanza of Heliodorus (1514) has the "Expulsion of Heliodorus from the Temple," "Miracle of Bolsena," "Leo I. and Attila," and the "Deliverance of S. Peter." In the Stanza Incendio del Borgo (1517), are the "Incendio del Borgo Vecchio," the "Justification of Leo III., before Charlemagne," the "Coronation of Charlemagne by Leo III.," and the "Victory of Leo IV. over the Saracens." Perino del Vaga (1500-47) and Giovanni da Udine (1494-1564) assisted Raphael in the last two paintings.

The Mural paintings for the Sala of Constantine, were designed and commenced by Raphael, but were carried out by his pupils, Giulio Romano (1492-1546), Francesco Penni (1488-1528), and Raffaelle del Colle. The Loggie of the Vatican, by Bramante, was also decorated by Raphael and his pupils. The then-recent discoveries of the baths of Titus and house of Livia, with their Roman Mural painting, influenced in a remarkable degree the decorative painting of the cinque-cento period. These arabesques —or as they were termed *grotteschi*, being found in the grottos of

61

Roman gardens—were utilised by Raphael in the decoration of the pilasters, piers, and walls of the Loggie. The designs were painted with a fine range of colour upon white ground, and enclosed within borders of modelled stucco ornaments. In the panels upon the ceiling, Raphael painted a series of fifty-two incidents of the Bible. These are spoken of as " Raphael's Bible." Raphael was assisted in this work by many contemporary artists and pupils; Giovanni da Udine, Giulio Romano, Francesco Penni, Perino del Vaga, and Primaticcio (1490-1580,) who completed the work after Raphael's death. These artists carried the traditions and methods to other parts of Italy. Giulio Romano executed some fine Mural paintings at the Villa Madama, Rome; and for Federigo Gonzaga, Duke of Mantua, he enriched with beautiful paintings and arabesques the Palazzo Ducale, and the Palazzo del Te. These arabesques were upon richly-coloured or parti-coloured grounds (see plates 86-9, " Grammar of Ornament," by Owen Jones).

Perino del Vaga carried the art to Genoa, where at the Palazzo Andrea Doria he executed many admirable examples of coloured arabesques (see plates 43-9, " Palast-Architakur, Genua ").

These painted arabesques show a great inventiveness and skilful combination of parts, but they are not to be compared with the refined and beautiful modelling, and harmonious composition of the contemporary carved reliefs by Andrea Sansovino (1460-1528), Jacopo Sansovino (1486-1570), Agostino Busti, Pietro Lombardo (1500), and his sons, Tullio and Antonio. These delicate reliefs have the traditional Roman acanthus, but treated with a refined feeling for modelling, and beauty and symmetry of line and mass.

In many examples, vases, masks, shields, and similar accessories are found in profusion (plate 19). The composition of the cinquecento ornament is usually symmetrical, the details being varied and interesting in the best examples; and whilst lacking the vigour and symbolism of the Lombardic and Byzantine styles, it excelled them in its absolute adaptation to architectural conditions, with perfection of design and craftsmanship.

Magnificent examples of decoration by Pinturicchio are in the Sala Piccolomini, Siena, and by Perugino in the Sala del Cambio, Perugia, where some of the earliest painted arabesques are upon a dark ground.

Andrea Mantegna (1431-1517) executed nine paintings or cartoons in tempera upon linen, representing the triumphs of Julius Cæsar, which are a portion of a frieze 9 ft. high and 80 ft. long, painted for Lodovico Gonzaga's Palace of S. Sebastian, at Mantua. They were purchased by Charles I., and are now at Hampton Court. An illustration of this frieze, from an engraving upon copper in the British Museum, is given here. It was also engraved on wood by Andrea Andreani in 1599.

THE TRIUMPH OF JULIUS CÆSAR. FRIEZE BY ANDREA MANTEGNA

To Mantegna is also ascribed the illustrations to the " Hypnerotomachia, or Dream of Poliphilus," printed in 1499, at Venice, by Aldus Manutius.

Good reproductions of many of these early illustrated books are given in the " Italian Book Illustrations," by A. W. Pollard, No. 12 of the Portfolio, December 1894; and in " The Decorative Illustration of Books," by Walter Crane.

The study of classical architecture was stimulated by the publication at Rome, in 1486, of the treatise by Vitruvius, an architect of the time of Augustus; an edition was also published at Florence in 1496, and at Venice in 1511. In 1570, Fra Giocondo, at Venice, published " The Five Books of Architecture," by Andrea Palladio (1518-80). Another treatise upon architecture, by Serlio (1500-52), was also published at Venice in 1537 and 1540.

Beautiful types of the Renascence decorative art were the Venetian well-heads, situated as they were in most of the public squares of Venice, and in many of the court-yards of her princely palaces. Designed with details of the most varied and beautiful character by such artists as Andrea Sansovino, Pietro Lombardo, and his sons Tullio and Antonio, the Venetian well-head became a type of beauty, diversified in its treatment, but never losing its characteristics or its usefulness. Venetian well-heads display a great variety of form and decoration, and are a tribute to the vivacity and artistic feeling of the Venetian Republic.

THE STROZZI PALACE, FLORENCE.

The Renascence in Italy was distinguished by the many magnificent ecclesiastical and secular buildings erected during the 15th and 16th centuries in the chief cities in Italy. Florence was the first to show activity, and with Brunelleschi (1377-1446), the history of Renascence architecture commences. The great dome of the Cathedral (1420-34), the Pazzi Chapel (with a fine frieze of cherubs' heads by Donatello and Settigiano) at S. Croce (1420), and the Church of S. Lorenzo (1425), were his first works, and were followed by S. Spirito (1433) and the Pitti Palace.

The severe dignity of the bold rusticated stone work, which was usually varied in each story, the circular-headed windows, and cornices of great depth and projection, became the type of the early palaces of Florence and Siena.

The first Renascence palace was the Riccardi, built for Cosimo de Medici, in 1430, by Michelozzi: and it was followed by the Pitti (1435) and the Quaratesi (1442), by Brunelleschi; the Rucellai (1451), by Leon Battista Alberti (1404-72), where pilasters with their entablature were used for the first time in a Renascence façade; the Strozzi (1489), by M. da Majano and Cronaca; the Gondi (1490), by G. da Sangallo; the Guadagni (1490), with *sgraffito* decorations in grey and white plaster; and the Nicolini, by Bramante (1444-1514); the Pandolfini (1520), by Raphael; and the Bartolini (1520), by Baccio d'Agnolo. The plan of these palaces was usually a rectangle, having an internal cortile, with open arcades on the ground floor, the next floor having windows, while the upper story was frequently open.

64

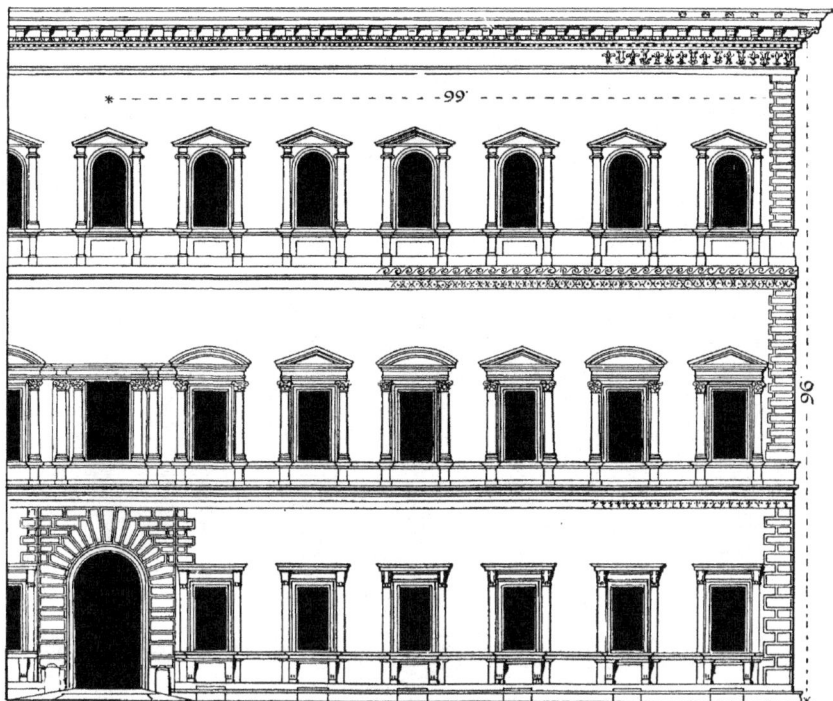

THE FARNESE PALACE, ROME.

In Rome the palaces were characterized by largeness of scale, the frequent use of the pilaster or attached super-imposed columns, and square-headed windows, with triangular or segmental pediments. The plan is rectangular, with a cortile of one or more stories of open arcades of semi-circular arches, springing direct from the capital, as in the Cancelleria Palace.

The chief palaces are the Cancelleria (1495) and the Giraud (1503), by Bramante (1444-1514); the Farnesina (1511), the Massimi (1529), and the Villa Ossoli (1525), by Baldassare Peruzzi (1481-1536); the Palma and the Farnese (1517), by Antonio Sangallo (1476-1546); the Villa Madama (1516), by Raffaello and Giulio Romano; the Borghese (1590), by Martino Lunghi; the Laterano (1586), by Fontana; and the Barberini (1626), by Maderna, Borromini, and Bernini.

The chief ecclesiastical building is S. Peter's (plan, plate 53,) commenced in 1450 by Alberti and Rossellino for Pope Nicolas V.; then carried on by Bramante and San Gallo (1503), Raphael and Peruzzi (1514-20), Antonio da San Gallo (1534), Michel Angelo (1546), Vignola (1556), Giacomo della Porta (1590), and Carlo Maderna (1608). In 1627 S. Peter's was dedicated by Urban VIII., and in 1667 the colonnade in the piazza was erected by Bernini.

THE PALAZZO VENDRAMINI, VENICE, BY PIETRO LOMBARDO.

The architecture of Venice is rich and varied in style, and the great *palazzi* of the Byzantine, Gothic, and Renascence periods bear tribute to the versatility and skill of the Venetian architects and craftsmen.

The Renascence period may be said to commence with Pietro Lombardo, who built Santa Maria dei Miracoli (1480), a building remarkable for the singular grace and refinement of the internal carved enrichments. Another work by Lombardo was the Spinelli Palace (1480), which has mullioned windows, grouped centrally as in the Gothic palace. This feature, together with the use of pilasters or attached columns, became the type of the later Renascence palaces, such as the Palazzo Vendramini, also by Pietro Lombardo. Then followed the rebuilding of the court-yard of the Ducal Palace by Antonio-Bregni (1485), which was completed in 1550 by Scarpagnino; the Scuolo di San Marco (1485) by Martino Lombardo; the Palazzo Cornaro (1532), La Zecca (1536), the Loggetta of the Campanile (1540), destroyed by the falling of the Campanile in 1905, and the Library of S. Mark (1536), by Jacopo Sansovino; the Grimani Palace (1549) by San Michel; the Pesaro Palace (1650) and the Church of Santa Maria della Salute (1631) by Baldassare Longhena.

66

51' 6"

61' 6"

PALAZZO VERZI, VERONA.

Andre Palladio (1518-80), of Vicenza, was the most famous of the later architects of the Renascence. His chief works are the Basilica Vicenza (1549), which has a fine elevation of two super-imposed orders of attached columns, with arched openings and coupled columns in each story; the Valmarana (1556), the Chiericati (1560), and the Tiene (1565) palaces; and the Teatro Olimpico (1580); all of which are in Vicenza.

In his later work, which is frequently built of brick and stucco, he adopted the device occasionally used by Peruzzi and San Michel, of an attached column, with or without pedestal, reaching throughout the two stories of the full height of the building, as in the Casa del Diavolo.

Scamozzi (1552-1616), of Vicenza, succeeded Palladio. He built the Trissino at Vicenza (1588), the Procuratie Nuove (1584) at Venice, and completed Palladio's Church of San Giorgio Maggiore at Venice.

CASA DEL DIAVOLO.

67

EARLY RENASCENCE SCREEN. CLUNY MUSEUM.

FRONT of COFFER PERIOD of LOUIS XII. CLUNY MUSEUM.

CARVED WOOD PANEL CLUNY MUSEUM

PANEL of DOOR St MACLOU, ROUEN. BY JEAN GOUJON

PANELS FROM LIMOGES CATHEDRAL.

FRENCH RENASCENCE.

It was just at the close of the 15th century that the influence of the Italian Renascence began to be felt upon the vigorous and beautiful Gothic art of France. At first this influence was confined to the ornament, while the chief constructive features were still of the traditional Gothic (plate 23); but early in the 16th century the French Renascence became a distinct style, uniting the vigour and the exuberance of the flamboyant carving, with the classical refinement of the Italian Renascence.

The monument to Charles VIII. (1499), the tomb of Francis, Duc de Bretagne, at Nantes, by Michel Colombe (1507), the tomb of Louis XII. at S. Denis, by Jean Just (1519-27), and the exterior of the choir and the north spire of Chartres Cathedral, by Jean Texier (1514-27), are fine examples of the transitional period.

With the advent of the Italians, Rosso and Primaticcio, to the court of Francis I., in 1530, the true French Renascence commences, and is usually divided into distinct periods, viz.:—1. François Premier, 1515-47; 2. Henri Deux and Henri Quatre, 1547-1610; 3. Louis Treize, 1610-43; 4. Louis Quatorze, 1643-1715; 5. Louis Quinze, 1715-74; 6. Louis Seize, 1774-89; and 7. The Empire, 1804-70.

FRANCOIS PREMIER.—This period is remarkable for the eminent Italians engaged by Francis I., in 1530, for the embellishment of the Château Fontainebleau. Here the Salle Francis I. is enriched with stucco and painted ornament by Primaticcio, and wood carving by Siebecqi. The details of the ornament, though Italian in character, still retain the squareness of the Gothic period, and are essentially French in feeling.

The châteaux were characteristic examples of the early architecture. That of Chambord (1526) has circular towers at the angles and flanking the entrance, with a roof of cones, cupolas, and high dormer windows and chimneys. A little later, pilasters were introduced, together with the square-mullioned window and the high dormer windows so characteristic of the earlier French Renascence. The Louvre was commenced by Pierre Lescot (1510-78), who built the southwest angle, and enriched with sculpture by Jean Goujon (1515-72), who also executed the beautiful Fontaine des Innocents at Paris, in 1550, with low relief panels of draped figures.

THE HENRI DEUX AND HENRI QUATRE.—The prevalence of interlaced strap work, delicate reliefs, and the use of the *cartouche*, are characteristics of this style, as seen in the Salle Henri II. at Fontainebleau, by Andronet du Cerceau. These features are also seen in the Oiron pottery (plate 35), the geometrical interlacings and arabesques of Grolier (plate 47), and the book illustrations of Orance Finé, and of Jean Cousin—whose versatility is shown by his designs

69

1

PANEL IN CARVED WOOD.

2

ROCOCO OR LOUIS QUINZE.
WOOD CARVING. NOTRE DAME.

3

4

TROPHIES OF ARMS BY GIRARDON. VERSAILLES.

for stained glass for Sainte Chapelle at Vincennes, and the fine statue of Admiral Chabot. Of the architecture of this period, the Tuileries was commenced in 1564 by Philibert de Lorme (1500-78), De Carreau and Duperie continued the Louvre, and the Luxembourg was built by De Brosse in 1611.

THE LOUIS TREIZE. — The beautiful tooled bindings by Nicolas and Clovis Eve (plate 47), and the delicate *pointelle* tooling by Le Gascon, are fine examples of the ornament of this period.

THE LOUIS QUATORZE.—The Palace of Versailles, by François (1598-1666) and Jules Mansard (1645-1708), is the great repertory of this period. It is enriched internally with coloured and gilded stucco, paintings by Le Brun (1619-90) and Mignard, magnificent Gobelins' tapestries, and decorative furniture of tortoise-shell and brass marquetry by André Boule. The beautiful Rouen pottery, the splendid woven fabrics of Lyons (plate 50), and the decorative compositions of Le Pautre, are some of the best examples of the period known as the *Barocque*. A fine example of the architecture is the colonnade and south front of the Louvre, by Claude Perrault (1666).

THE LOUIS QUINZE.—The *Rococo*, introduced in 1725 by Gilles Marie Oppenord, was paramount in this period, and the ornament was composed of the scroll, shell, and flowers, showing no restraint or reticence in composition or in detail. Symmetry was avoided, and brilliancy and playfulness of effect were sought for (plate 24). The pastoral scenes by the painter Watteau (1684-1721), and the fine inlaid furniture made by Jean François Ochen (1754-68) for Madame de Pompadour, are some of the better examples of this period.

THE LOUIS SEIZE is distinguished by its severity of line and reticence of detail. Room decorations were frequently in white and gold, with refined and delicately-painted or stucco ornament. Painted panels by Fragonard and Boucher, and marquetry furniture by Riesener and David Roentgen, with bronze or ormolu mountings by Gouthiére, were executed for the court of Queen Marie Antoinette. S. Geneviève (the Pantheon) by Soufflot (1755-81) represents the architecture.

THE EMPIRE.—Purely classical forms and enrichments prevailed, more pretentious perhaps, but lacking the beauty, refinement, and vitality of the Louis Seize.

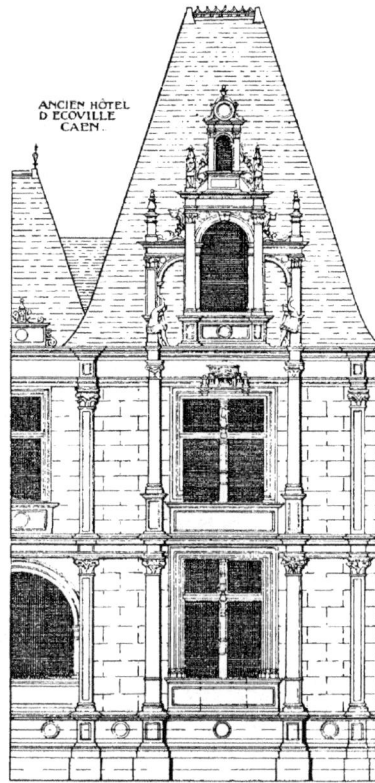

71

DESIGN FOR
A TIME-METRE.
BY HOLBEIN. 1544

CANOPY TO STALLS
ST CROSS, WINCHESTER
1528

WOODCARVING, ASTON HALL

PORTION OF
CEILING AT
ASTON HALL,
BIRMINGHAM.

PORTION OF HENRY VII TOMB
BY TORRIGIANO
WESTMINSTER
ABBEY

PANEL FROM THE CHICHESTER TOMB, PILTON CHURCH, DEVON
1566

STONE CARVING. CREWE HALL CHESHIRE.

ENGLISH RENASCENCE.

The Renascence commenced in England in the early part of the 16th century, about a hundred years later than in Florence. The first important work was the tomb of John Young, in terra cotta, in the Rolls' Chapel, completed in 1516 by Pietro Torrigiano, who also executed the fine tomb of Henry VII. (1512-18) in Westminster Abbey. This consists of a rectangular sarcophagus of black marble, on which rest the bronze effigies of the king and his consort. On the sarcophagus are gilded bronze pilasters and circular panels in relief, surrounded with wreaths of black marble (plate 25). The tomb of Margaret, Countess of Richmond, and the high altar, and baldachino of black and white marble in the Abbey are also by Torrigiano.

Contemporary with Torrigiano was Benedetto da Rovezzano, of Florence, who was commissioned by Cardinal Wolsey, in 1520, to make a sarcophagus of black touch-stone, with a recumbent figure of Wolsey in bronze. On the Cardinal's fall, Henry VIII. commissioned Rovezzano to alter and elaborate the work ; but it was left incomplete, and in 1646 the bronze was sold, and this sarcophagus became the resting-place of Nelson in 1806, and is now in S. Paul's Cathedral. Another Florentine, Giovanni di Majano, modelled some terra-cotta medallions for Wolsey at Hampton Court (1521).

In the work of Hans Holbein (1488-1554, plate 25) the Italian feeling is still retained, showing but little of the Gothic tradition ; but in the middle of the century there came a marked change in the ornamental details, the cartouche and strap work, features common to the later French, Flemish, and German Renascence, becoming a pronounced feature of the English Renascence (plate 25).

The chief buildings of the early Renascence are Charlecote (1558), Longleat (1567), Kirby Hall (1570-75), Montacute House (1580), Wollaton Hall (1580-88), Hardwicke Hall, and Haddon Hall (1592-97). Of the Jacobean period there are Holland House (1607), Hatfield (1611), Audley End (1616), Aston Hall (1620), and Blickling Hall (1620), with their long galleries and rectangular mullioned windows—characteristic features of the Elizabethan and Jacobean period. There are magnificent circular bay windows at Kirby Hall, Burton Agnes (1602-10), and Lilford Hall (1635), and fine octagonal bays at Astley Hall.

The beautiful plaster ceilings, consisting of geometrical panelling, fan-tracery, and pendentives were similar to those of the preceding Gothic period. These richly-moulded pendentives were connected together with bands of pierced strap-work, or moulded ribs with arabesques in low relief. From 1615 to 1650 the panels were composed of purely geometrical forms, such as circles, squares, lozenges, and interlacing quatrefoils, with delicate arabesques. The

CARVED PANEL FROM THE CHURCH OF ST MARY, BUILT BY WREN, 1695. SOUTH KENSINGTON MUSEUM.

FRIEZE FROM THE CHOIR STALLS, ST PAUL'S.

PANEL IN STONE. NORTH PORCH. ST PAUL'S CATHEDRAL.

DOOR-HEAD. CLIFFORDS INN.

DOOR-HEAD FROM CLIFFORDS INN.

FRIEZE OF THE UPPER ORDER OF THE BANQUETING HOUSE, WHITEHALL. BY INIGO JONES. 1622.

CARVED FIRE-PLACE IN OAK & CEDAR, FROM A ROOM AT CLIFFORDS INN, LONDON. 1686. NOW IN THE SOUTH KENSINGTON MUSEUM.

ribs frequently had a repeating pattern impressed while the plaster was soft. Occasionally a double frieze was used, the lower having delicate arabesques and strap-work, while the upper one had boldly-marked cartouches and arabesques. One of the most important examples of early Renascence plaster is the frieze in the presence chamber, Hardwicke Hall. It is decorated with classical subjects, such as Diana and her nymphs, surrounded with forest trees and foliage. This frieze is 11 ft. in height, modelled in low relief, delicately coloured, and is probably the work of Charles Williams.

With Inigo Jones (1573-1652) the purely Italian Renascence prevailed. He was known from 1604-30 as the designer for the elaborate scenery for the brilliant masques by Ben Jonson that were performed by the nobles and court of that period. In 1622 Inigo Jones completed the Banqueting House, Whitehall, the only portion of his great design which was carried out. He also designed the Water Gate, York House, executed by his favourite carver, Nicholas Stone, the earlier part of Greenwich Hospital, and the great room at Wilton, with its fine mantelpiece and panelling.

Nicholas Stone was an expert and prolific carver. An extract from his pocket-book is interesting, and throws some light on the cost of sculpture:—" 1620. I made a monument, to be set up at Westminster, of Mr. Francis Holles, the youngest son of the earl of Clare, for which the sayd earl payed for it 50*l.* My lord of Clare also agreed with me for a monument for his brother, Sir George Holles, the which I made and sett up in the chappell at Westminster where Sir Francis Vere lyeth buried, for the which I was payed from the hands of the sayd earl of Clare 100*l.*"

The ornament of Inigo Jones is excellent in proportion, and Italian in type. The decoration of the panels and friezes consisted of boldly-designed festoons, masks, and shields. The plaster ceilings have large rectangular, circular, or oval panels, with moulded ribs enriched with arabesques, fruit, or flowers in high relief.

The work of Wren, which followed, is on similar lines, the proportions being good, but the details are less refined in type, being largely under the influence of Grinling Gibbons and his school. Their wonderful technique and lack of restraint in the hands of less able men degenerated into the mannerisms and looseness of style which marked the later 17th and early 18th centuries.

The era of church building began with Sir Christopher Wren (1632-1723) in 1666, after the great fire of London, in which old S. Paul's, ninety-three parish churches and chapels, the Exchange, the Guildhall, and fifty of the City Companies' halls were destroyed. S. Mary-le-Bow (1680), S. Bride's (1680), S. Clement Dane (1684), and S. Stephen's, Walbrook, illustrate some of the typical features of the fifty-one parochial churches that he designed, and his masterpiece, S. Paul's (1675-1710), is a noble example of English Renascence (plan, plate 53). Wren also built portions of Hampton Court

LIBRARY
CEILING
BY THE
BROTHERS
ADAM.

SPANDRIL OF
BRONZE STOVE-GRATE
BY ALFRED STEVENS.

DOOR PANEL BY
ROBERT ADAM.

BORDERS BY GODFREY SYKES.

and Greenwich Hospital. Hawksmoor (1661-1736), a pupil of Wren, built Christ Church, S. George's-in-the-East (1723), Spitalfields Church (1729), and S. George's, Bloomsbury (1730). Castle Howard (1714) and Blenheim Palace are by Vanbrugh (1666-1726); S. Philip, Birmingham (1710), by Archer; Burlington House (1717) by Campbell, who also brought out his great work on English architecture, "Vitruvius Britannicus," Vol. I., 1715, Vol. II., 1717, Vol. III., 1725, while Vols. IV. and V. were issued by Woolfe and Gandon in 1767. This book gives introductory descriptions, with plans, elevations, and sections of the chief English buildings erected between 1600-1750. The Horse Guards (1742), Holkham (1734), and Devonshire House (1734) were designed by Kent. S. Mary-le-Strand (1717), S. Martin's (1721), the Senate House, Cambridge (1730), and the Radcliffe Library (1747) were by Gibbs (1682-1754).

With Chambers (1726-96) the later Renascence begins, and Somerset House (1776) is a typical example of this period, accurate in proportion, with refined details and excellent workmanship and materials. Chambers also published his "Treatise of Civil Architecture" in 1759, and "A Treatise on the Decorative Part of Civil Architecture" in 1791.

Other architects of this period were George Dance, who built the Mansion House (1756), and Robert and James Adam, who designed and built the Adelphi (1768) and many streets and mansions in London, Bath, Edinburgh, and Dublin. Robert Adam also designed many accessories, such as console tables and candelabra, and on the ceilings, pilasters, and panels were classical stucco enrichments (plate 26). Pergolese, Bartolozzi, and Angelica Kaufmann contributed designs and paintings for the brothers Adam.

Of modern Renascence, the Wellington Monument, in S. Paul's Cathedral, by Alfred Stevens (1818-75), is distinguished by its strong personality and architectonic treatment of composition, and the beauty and singular grace of its details.

RELIEF ORNAMENT FROM THE WEKALA CAIRO.
ARABIAN 15TH CENTURY.

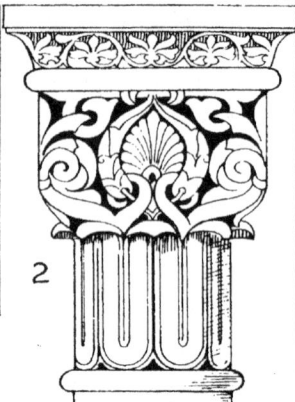

CAPITAL FROM THE COURT OF
THE LIONS, ALHAMBRA

FRIEZE, IN MOSQUE OF SULTAN HASAN CAIRO 14TH CENTURY
FROM THE ART OF THE SARACENS

CEILING DECORATION, FROM
THE ALHAMBRA MORESQUE.

WALL DECORATION FROM THE ALHAMBRA SPAIN.   MORESQUE. (OWEN JONES.

AHOMETAN ORNAMENT.

Of mediæval history as associated with the decorative arts, the rise and development of the Arabs is the most remarkable. The wide appreciation and liberal patronage of the arts by the Khalifs; the influence of its religion and precepts upon contemporary and later periods of art; the distinct individuality and geometrical arrangement of its ornamentation; all had a most marked effect upon tradition and craftmanship.

The history commences with Mohammed, A.D. 570-632, who founded and consolidated the empire, of which, under Omar, A.D. 635, Damascus became the capital; in A.D. 638 Kufa and Bassora were founded in Persia. In A.D. 641 Egypt was conquered, and the Mahometan capital, Fustât, founded. Persia was conquered in A.D. 642, Spain invaded in A.D. 711, Bagdad in Persia became the capital of the Arabian Khalifs in A.D. 762, and in A.D. 827 Sicily was conquered; but it was not until the dynasty of Ibn-Tūlūn, A.D. 878-914, that the history of Cairene art begins, of which the mosque of Ibn-Tūlūn in Fustât, or old Cairo, is the earliest example. Under the Fatimy dynasty, A.D. 867-1171, Cairo was founded, and the arts, receiving further encouragement, were now introducd into Sicily and Europe. In A.D. 997 the Mahometan invasion of India took place. In A.D. 796-965 the mosque of Cordova was built, and in A.D. 1236 the kingdom of Grenada was founded and the Alhambra was built, by Mohammed ben Alhamar, A.D. 1248, and Mahometan art, as exemplified in architectural decorations, arms and armour, woodwork, ivory, textile fabrics and illuminated books, reached its culmination under the Mamlūk dynasty, A.D. 1250-1516.

Thus the Arabs, from a roving tribe, became, by religious zeal and conquests, the most powerful and wealthiest nation of mediæval times, assimilating and influencing the customs and the arts of the different nations and provinces.

The term MAHOMETAN ART includes ARABIAN, MORESQUE, PERSIAN, INDIAN, and SICILIAN, all having the same characteristics, yet distinguished by the racial influence and custom. The Arabian is marked by its flowing, interlacing, and symmetrical lines, geometrical arrangement (doubtless derived from Byzantine sources), and its prevalence of inscriptions or texts from the Koran. In Spain a more complex geometrical arrangement is found, intermingled with a flowing foliage or arabesque of a purely conventional type. This style is noticeable for its entire absence of any natural forms and its abundant use of inscriptions and glazed and enamelled tiles, distinctly influenced by Persian tradition, though purely geometric and formal. These tiles cover the lower part of the wall, the upper portion, as also the ceiling, being decorated with arabesques of modelled plaster in flat relief, of two or more planes, enriched with red, blue, white, and gold; this is typical of the Moresque style. The Sicilian work is remarkable for its beautiful fabrics of silk and the prevalence in its ornament of birds, animals, and heraldic forms, showing the continuity of the traditions of Persia (plate 49 and page 142).

PLATE.
SILICEOUS GLAZED EARTHENWARE. RHODIAN. 15 & 16ᵗʰ Century
WHITE GROUND. RED FLOWERS. BLUE & GREEN FOLIAGE.

HOOKER BASE. GLAZED EARTHENWARE WITH
ARABESQUE ORNAMENT 16ᵗʰ OR 17ᵗʰ CENTURY.

EARTHENWARE PLATE. 16ᵗʰ CENTURY
BLUE GROUND. WHITE & GREEN FLOWERS & FOLIAGE.

BLUE WHITE & GREEN WALL TILES

RHODIAN TILE. WHITE ORNAMENT ON RED GROUND. THE DARK PART DEEP BLUE
15ᵗʰ OR 16ᵗʰ CENTURY

TILE FROM CAIRO. RHODIAN. 16ᵗʰ CENTURY. BLUE GROUND.

BLUE AND GREEN TILE. FROM DAMASCUS

PERSIAN ORNAMENT.

The early art of Persia was similar to that of Assyria and Babylon, having the same forms, materials, and traditions. With the accession of the Sassanides, A.D. 223, came the introduction of the elliptical dome, so typical of eastern architecture. This dome rested on pendentives, which occupied the angles of the square base. These pendentives and the elliptical dome are distinctive features in Mahometan architecture.

The industrial arts of Persia were largely influenced by the traditional arts of Assyria and Chaldea. This tradition was carried on with rare skill and selective power by the Persians, culminating in the splendid period of Shah Abbas, A.D. 1586-1625. The vitality, beauty, and interest of detail, combined with perfect decorative adaptation to material, are characteristic of the textiles, pottery, metal work, and illuminated manuscripts of the 15th, 16th, and 17th centuries.

The Mahometan conquest of Persia, A.D. 632-637, by Abu Bekr, the successor of Mohammed, largely influenced the development of the arts of the Persians, who adopted the customs and habits of contemporary races, yet preserved all the characteristics of their art; and there is no doubt that the art of the Arabs was founded upon the traditional arts of Persia.

Persian decoration is characterised by a fine feeling for form and colour, and for the singularly frank renderings of natural plants, such

PERSIAN PLATE. 16TH CENTURY. S.K.M.

as the pink, hyacinth, tulip, rose, iris, and the pine and date. These are used with perfect sincerity and frankness, and are essentially decorative in treatment, combining harmony of composition of mass, beauty of form, and purity of colour. It was doubtless owing to these qualities, together with the perfect adaptation of ornament to material, that the Persian style so largely influenced contemporary work, and especially the European textile fabrics of the 16th and 17th centuries. The illustrations given are of some familiar types of Persian adaptations of natural flowers, doubtless chosen for their significance, beauty of growth and form, and appropriateness of decorative treatment. Purely Arabian forms, as given in plate 28, are frequently associated with the Persian floral treatment, showing the influence of the artists of Damascus. Many fine examples of lustred wall tiles, dating from the 10th and 11th centuries, are in the South Kensington Museum, of which the blue, brown, and turquoise colouring is of a splendid quality. They often have Arabic inscriptions interspersed with the floral enrichments. Examples of wall tiles of the 8th century have been found in the ruins of Rhages.

These lustred tiles are a remarkable instance of tradition or hereditary proclivity. This art, beginning with the enamelled bricks of Babylon, and the later frieze of Susa (page 17) with its brilliant enamel and fine colour, was continued by the Persians, and, passing to the Arabs, the tradition was carried to Cairo, Spain, and Majorca; thence into Italy, where enamelled lustre ware was made, differing from the original Persian in its frequent absence of utility, which was fundamental to the art of the Persians.

Mahometan ornament has five broad divisions, viz., Arabian, Sicilian, Moresque, Indian, and Persian; and they are all characterised by strongly-marked compartments or fields, which are filled with finer and more delicate enrichments. These compartments are most pronounced in the Moresque, with its complex geometric interlacing and entire absence of natural forms (figs. 4, 6, 7, and 8, plate 27). The Arabian style is somewhat similar, but less formal. The Indian has a conventional rendering of plants, and the introduction of the lion, tiger, and the elephant (fig. 2, plate 30); while in the Persian work there is a still less formal constructive arrangement, with floral forms clearly defined in line and mass, and the introduction of the human figure with the horse, the lion, the tiger, and birds. Note the illustration in Textiles, which is taken from a fine carpet in the South Kensington Museum. In this carpet, animal forms, chosen with rare selective power and judgment, are combined with the typical floral enrichment of Persia, with the wealth of colour, admirable detail of spacing and mass, beauty of incident and vigour, and appropriateness of treatment. These are features that distinguish the industrial designs of Persia; and it is doubtless due to the interest and vitality of their ornament that we owe the remarkable influence of Persian art upon the contemporary and latter craftsmanship of Europe.

←----- 12 INCHES -----→

←----- 12 INCHES -----→

2

3

WHITE PATTERN ON RED GROUND.
GENOESE FROM A PERSIAN DESIGN. S.K.M.

4

FROM A PERSIAN DRAWING
SOUTH KENSINGTON MUSEUM.

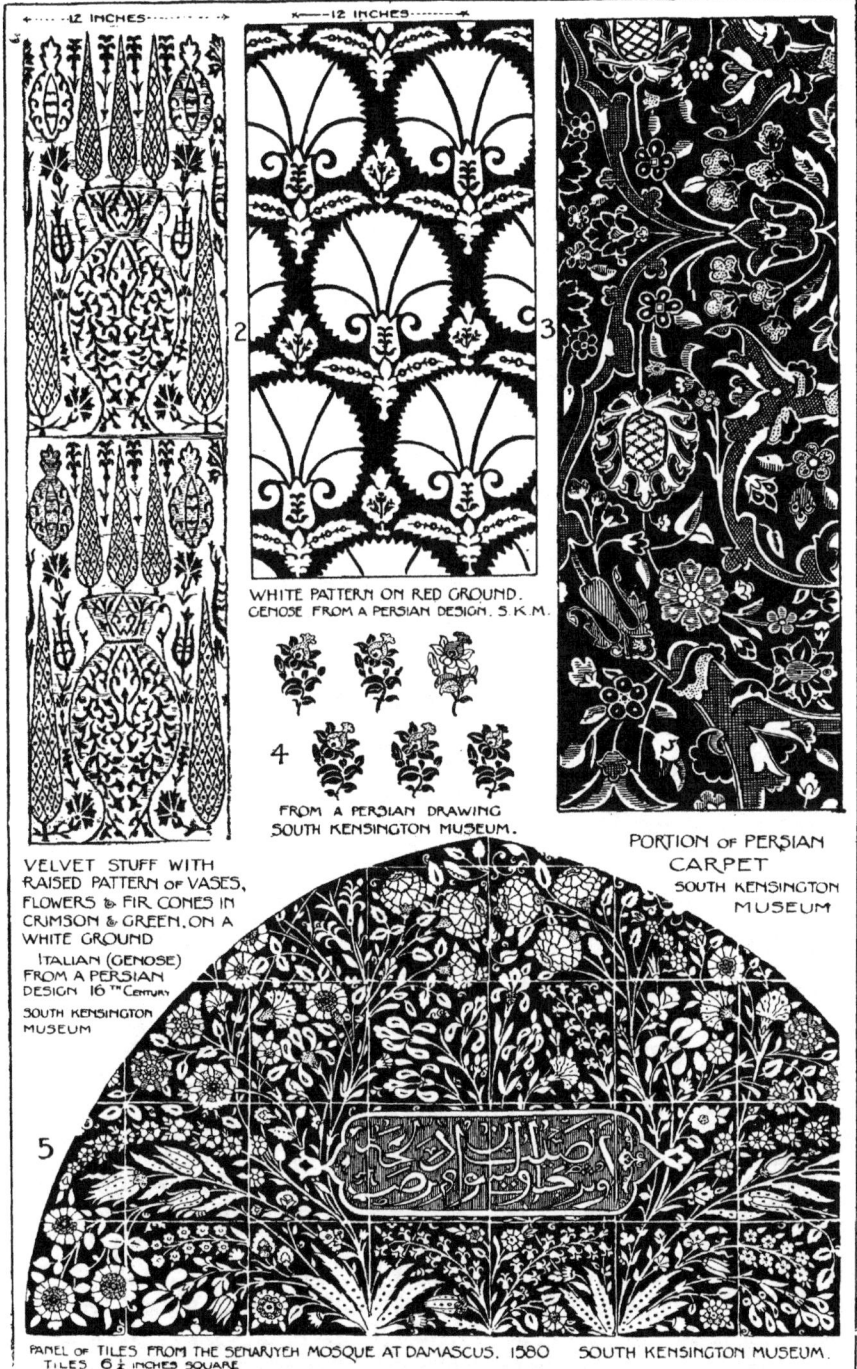

VELVET STUFF WITH
RAISED PATTERN OF VASES,
FLOWERS & FIR CONES IN
CRIMSON & GREEN, ON A
WHITE GROUND
ITALIAN (GENOESE)
FROM A PERSIAN
DESIGN 16 TH CENTURY
SOUTH KENSINGTON
MUSEUM

PORTION OF PERSIAN
CARPET
SOUTH KENSINGTON
MUSEUM

5

PANEL OF TILES FROM THE SENANIYEH MOSQUE AT DAMASCUS. 1580   SOUTH KENSINGTON MUSEUM.
TILES 6¼ INCHES SQUARE

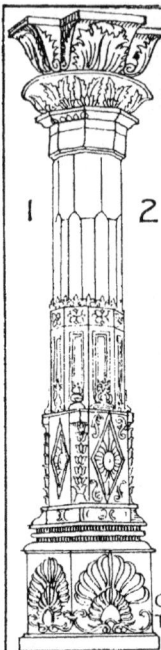

WOVEN FABRIC
BENARES. S.K.M.

COLUMN FROM
TEMPLE OF VISHA.
BENARES.

PRINTED COTTON. BOCK COLLECTION.
MANCHESTER.

SILK BROCADE WITH PINE SHAPED
FLOWERS. BENARES. S.K.M.

COTTON PRINT WITH FLOWERS IN
THE FORM OF A LEAF. S.K.M.

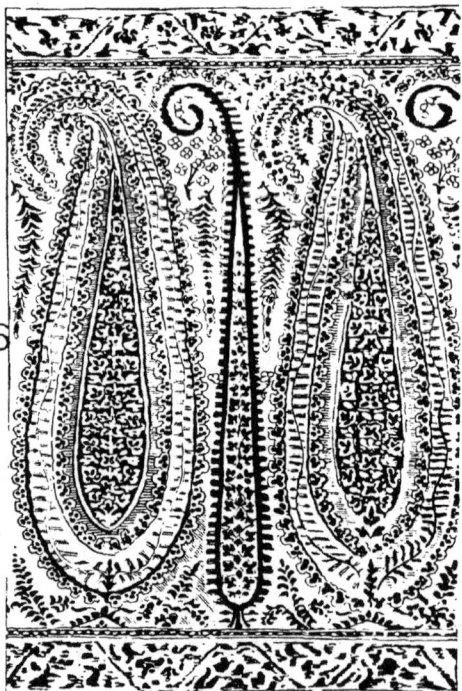

CASHMERE SCARF WITH THE PATTERN
FORMED OF PINES SCARLET GROUND. S.K.M.

INDIAN ORNAMENT.

The civilization of India dates from the remote past, but the oldest remains of its art and architecture are connected with the Buddhist religion, introduced by the prophet Sakya Muni (638 B.C.). This influenced the arts of India till A.D. 250, when the Jaina style was adopted. The examples of Buddhist architecture consist of Topes (which were sacred or monumental temples, either detached or rock-cut), and monasteries. The rock-cut temples usually consist of a nave and aisles, and a semi-circular recess containing a statue of the seated Buddha. The hall has square or octagonal columns, with bracket capitals (fig. 1). The finest examples of these temples are those at Ajanta, which are richly decorated in colour with incidents of Hindoo mythology. The fine temples at Ellora, which are cut entirely out from the rock, are of the Jaina period (A.D. 250). The pagodas at Chedombaram are of the Brahmin period, as is also the great hall of 1,000 pillars, which is 190 by 340 ft., containing the sacred image of the god Siva.

Alexander the Great conquered India 327 B.C., and doubtless left the influence of the Persian tradition in India. This influence was still further developed by the commercial intercourse of Persia and India, and by the Arabian invasion of India in A.D. 711, when a Mahometan dynasty was established (711-1152). This largely controlled and influenced the arts under the Mogul dynasty (1525-1837), when the decorative arts and the manufacture of the beautiful woven brocades and silks were fully developed. The splendid carpets and rugs, printed cottons, metal work, and fine enamels of this dynasty bear a remarkable tribute to the vitality, originality of ideas, and the practical utility of the industrial arts of India.

Indian ornament has the typical Mahometan division of spaces, but is more flowing and graceful than the pure Arabian style. These divisions are filled with fine conventional floral forms, such as the lotus, the date or hom, the iris, the rosette, and the pine. This pine is treated occasionally as a single flower, but more frequently as a cluster of flowers, which still retains the distinctive form of the pine (figs. 2, 4, and 6).

Typical also of this period is the judicious treatment of the elephant, lion, tiger, peacock, and the human figure, as accessories in the decorative arts of India. They were applied with rare knowledge and skill, combined with an artistic perception of applied art, and show a very strong affinity with contemporary Persian ornament.

Indian ornament has a more conventional rendering of natural forms than the frank treatment of Persian ornament. Block printing upon silk and cotton fabrics reached a high degree of perfection during the last century. The inventiveness and significance of detail, the charm of composition of line and mass, and the beautiful colour of these printed fabrics, are a reflex of the decorative feeling for beauty by the people of India.

WOVEN SILK CHINESE 18TH CENTURY
1 BOCK COLLECTION. MANCHESTER.

2 WOVEN SILK CHINESE 18TH CENTURY
BOCK COLLECTION. MANCHESTER

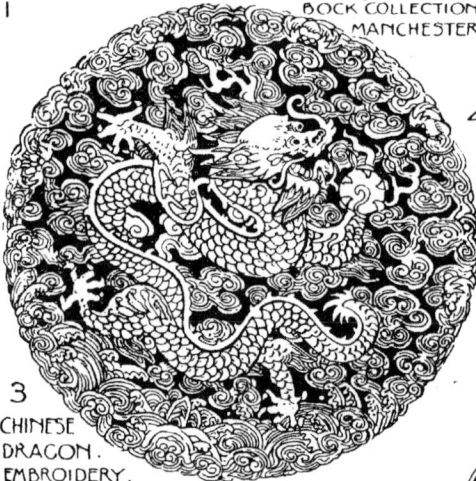

4 CHINESE DRAGON

3 CHINESE DRAGON. EMBROIDERY.

PAINTED BORDERS. MING DYNASTY. A.D 1358.

PAINTED PORCELAIN. 15TH CENTURY

CHINESE ORNAMENT.

The early bronzes, enamels, porcelain, and textile fabrics of China are indicative of the perfection and luxuriance of the decorative arts of that ancient empire. This perfection is shown by a splendid technique and a fine appreciation of colour and ornamentation, differentiated from the western nations by myths, traditions, and the remarkable persistency of a few typical forms through many centuries, doubtless owing to the profound ancestral worship and veneration for the past. The dragon was represented under many aspects, frequently forming vigorous lines of composition (figs. 3, 4). The beautiful flora of the country largely influenced Chinese art. The peony and chrysanthemum (frequently highly conventionalized) are typical examples, forming the elements of decorative design. Geometric forms, such as the hexagon, octagon, and the circle, enriched with flowers or the fret, are largely used. The many splendid examples of bells, gongs, and incense-burners in bronze and iron ; the carvings in wood, ivory, and jade ; the beautiful woven silks, richly patterned with the conventional chrysanthemum, the peony (fig. 2), or with geometrical forms, filled with the fret or rosettes (fig. 1) ; the magnificent fabrics, embroidered with dragons, birds, and conventional flowers, excellent in technique and colour ; and the richness and purity of their porcelain, more especially the old blue and white of the Ming dynasty, A.D. 1568-1640 (plate 36, fig. 4), all testify to the versatility and vitality of the Chinese decorative arts in the past.

Their architecture was distinguished by complexity and quaintness of form, rather than beauty of proportion and detail. Their pagodas, or temples, of which numerous examples are still extant, were of wood, iron, brick, or marble ; and one, the Nanking Pagoda, A.D. 1412-31, destroyed in 1854, was encased with yellow and green porcelain tiles, and had 150 bells pendant from the roof. Pagodas are from 3 to 13 stories in height; that at Peking has 13 stories and is 275 ft. high, the Nanking porcelain pagoda was 250 ft. high, and a fine brick one of 7 stories on the River Yangtsze is 140 ft. in height.

BASE OF SMALL PAGODA. CANTON

The roof of each story curves outwards and upwards, and usually supports a balcony. An illustration is given here of the lower story of the small pagoda at Canton, which is richly carved with figures and floral forms.

87

THE QUICK POSTMAN, FROM THE MANGWA, OR ROUGH SKETCHES. BY HOKUSAI. 1760-1849

CRANES.
PAINTED BY MORI IPPŌ,
1840. BRITISH MUSEUM.

WOVEN SILKS.

THE KIRI-MON & KIRU IMPERIAL CRESTS.

JAPANESE ORNAMENT.

The arts of Japan, though doubtless owing their origin to China, are differentiated by a keener observation of nature and a more literal treatment of landscape, bird and animal life, and the beautiful flora of the country—the "kiku" or chrysanthemum, the "botan" or peony, the "kosai" or iris, the "yuri" or lily, the "kiri" or paulawina imperialis (somewhat resembling our horse chestnut), the "matsu" or fir, and the "take" or bamboo—likewise the peacock, the crane, the duck, the pheasant, and many smaller beautiful birds, together with reptiles, insects, and fishes; all are elements in the decorative arts, being rendered with remarkable fidelity and delicacy of touch, united with a fine feeling for composition of line.

Physical phenomena, such as the snow-clad mountain, Fujiyama, have always exercised considerable influence upon the Japanese mind. This may be readily seen in the thirty colour prints by Hiroshige, and the hundred views of this mountain by Hokusai. The cherry and plum blossoms, emblems of the beauty and purity of spring, are also intimately associated with the life and the ornament of the people. It is this literal treatment of natural types, the marvellous technique, and especially the significance of the forms chosen, that constitutes the charm of the earlier Japanese art. It is singular that the materials used by the Japanese should be of little intrinsic value. Having no jewellery, they use little of the precious metals; iron, bronze, enamels, clay, wood, and lac being the chief materials utilized in the decorative arts of Japan. Bronze is one of the earliest materials used in the arts of Japan, and their large statue of Buddha at Kamakura, cast in A.D. 748, rests upon a lotus flower with fifty-six petals, 10 ft. by 6 ft., and the height from base to top of figure is 63 ft.

Pottery made but little development until the 13th century, when a coloured earthenware, having but little decoration, was produced at Seto, in Owari, and it was not until 1513 that porcelain was introduced from China into Arita, by Shondzui; and at the commencement of the 17th century a fine porcelain, decorated with birds and flowers in blue, red, and gold, now known as "Old Japan" or "Old Hizen," was produced. Kioto, Seto, and Arita were also noted for the production of a fine blue-and-white porcelain.

Cloisonné enamels, introduced in the 17th century, reached a high degree of technical excellence, but never quite reached the beauty, purity, and harmony of colour that characterized the old Chinese cloisonné.

Lacquer, of which some fine examples are reputed to date from the 7th century, was at its best in 1490 and 1709, when some beautiful examples with raised gold on a gold ground, or gold or silver foil on silver, black, or red grounds, were produced.

Japanese ornament frequently consists of the irregular distribution of powderings, or circular and fan-shaped medallions, often overlapping, or of hexagonal or honeycomb diapers and fret patterns.

Plate 33.

ROMAN SCROLL FROM THE FORUM OF TRAJAN.

PART II.
The Applied Arts.

WOODCUT FROM THE GROTESQUE ALPHABET OF 1464
(FLEMISH), BRITISH MUSEUM.

ENGRAVED PANEL BY HEINRICH ALDEGREVER, ONE OF THE
LITTLE MASTERS OF GERMANY.

BYZANTINE WALL MOSAIC COLOURED ORNA-
MENT on GOLD GROUND Sᵗ MARK'S VENICE·

ROMAN PAVEMENT. 2ᴺᴰ CENTURY VATICAN ROME

3

WALL MOSAIC OF COLOURED MARBLES
ARABIAN. 14ᵀᴴ CENTURY S.K.M.

MOSAIC FLOOR. ROMAN. FOUND AT ROME.

MARBLE INLAY ITALIAN. 15ᵀᴴ CENTURY
CHURCH OF Sᵗ JACOPO. FLORENCE

ROMAN PAVEMENT
IN RED, WHITE & BLACK
MARBLE FOUND IN 1795
NEAR LINCOLN.

MOSAICS.

Mosaic is the art of forming patterns by means of pieces of variously-coloured materials, fitted together, and is broadly divided into *Opus Tesselatum*, of small cubes, like dice; *Opus Sectile*, of slices of marble; and *Opus Musivum*, or glass mosaic: and may be subdivided into *Opus Figinum*, or ceramic mosaic; *Opus Vermiculatum*, with (*a*) *majus*, black and white marble; (*b*) *medium*, all materials and colours; and (*c*) *minus*, of minute tesseræ, used for furniture inlay. *Opus Alexandrinum* is an inlay of porphyry and serpentine on white marble.

It was in Rome that the art of mosaic was brought to its greatest perfection. The finest example is from the House of the Faun, Pompeii, and represents the battle of Issus, between Alexander and Darius. This mosaic, of the 3rd century B.C., is probably a copy of a Greek painting. A magnificent example of this period is the so-called "Pliny's Doves," a representation of four doves upon a basin.

Many fine Roman mosaics have been found in England, at Cirencester, London, Lincoln (fig. 6), Leicester, and at Brading.

Magnificent examples of *Opus Misivum* are found at Ravenna, Constantinople, and Venice, where the *Opus Muisvum* reached its culmination. Of the Ravenna (page 31) mosaics, those of the Baptistery, A.D. 450, S. Apollinare, and S. Vitale are typical examples of the earlier Byzantine mosaics, having dark green and blue backgrounds, with tesseræ about ⅜ in. square. The beautiful frieze of male and female saints in S. Apollinare extends along both sides of the nave, and is 10 ft. high. The vaulting and domes of S. Mark are entirely covered with the characteristic 11th century Byzantine gold ground mosaic, formed by fusing two pieces of glass together with gold leaf between. At Santa Sophia, Constantinople, and in the Cappella Palatina, Palermo, are other fine early mosaics.

Splendid examples of *Opus Alexandrinum* are found on the pavement of the Pantheon, Rome (A.D. 118-38). Other examples, dating from the 8th century, are in Rome, in the nave of the Basilica of San Lorenzo fuori le Mura, having interlacing circular bands of geometrical mosaic on white marble. In Santa Maria in Trastevere, the pattern is formed of hexagons and stars of six or eight points. A beautiful design of a large eight-pointed star of porphyry, with the triangles between the points of the star filled with small geometric *Opus Alexandrinum*, is in the Church of S. S. Giovanni e Paolo.

In the 13th and 14th centuries in Italy, the Cosmati (a family of mosaicists) produced some fine geometrical inlaid mosaics upon the vertical and twisted pillars in the cloisters of San Giovanni Laterano, and on the splendid "Ambone," or pulpit, in Santa Maria, in Araceli, Rome. On the tombs of Edward (A.D. 1270) and Henry III. (1280), in Westminster Abbey, are some good examples of this "Cosmati" mosaic.

93

TYPICAL FORMS OF GREEK VASES

HYDRIA.
FOR CARRYING
WATER.

CRATER.
FOR MIXING WINE
AND WATER.

CANTHAROS.
WINE CUP.

AMPHORA.
FOR CARRYING
WINE.

OINOCHOE.
FOR POURING
WINE.

LEKYTHOS.
FOR
POURING
OIL

KYLIX.
WINE CUP.

No 2.3.4
5.6 & 7
FROM THE
MANCHESTER
COLLECTION.

DANCING FIGURES FROM AN AMPHORA B.C. 400.

2

OINOCHOE B.C. 600.

3

TWO-HANDLED
VASE. ŒDIPUS.
JOCASTA. AND
THE SPHINX. B.C. 400.
RED FIGURED PERIOD

4

OINOCHOE, OR WATER JUG.
B.C. 500.

5

AMPHORA
BLACK
FIGURED
PERIOD. B.C. 500.

6

LEKYTHOS.
RED FIGURED
PERIOD.

7

RED FIGURED PERIOD.

KYLIX
B.C. 400.

GREEK CERAMICS.

It is difficult in modern times to realise the importance of vases in ancient times. To the Greeks a vase was a receptacle for food or liquid, and was used for the adornment of the home; it was used in the daily life of the living, and buried with the dead. Most of the finer vases found in Etruscan tombs are of Greek workmanship, imported from Greece or Grecian colonies; some black unglazed Etruscan vases have been found, but painted vases of Etruscan origin are rare.

Early Greek pottery, dating probably from the 10th century B.C., has been found in Greece, the colonies of Rhodes, Cyrene in Africa, and Naucratis in the delta of Egypt. These, showing a historic development, are arranged in groups, each with its distinctive characteristic. (1st) PRIMITIVE VASES, simple in shape, handles small or absent, decorations in simple line, punctured or incised, or in raised slip. (2nd) MYCENÆ or COLONIAL (B.C. 900-700) vases, often covered with a creamy slip, the designs, painted in brown and black, being derived from geometric patterns with marine and animal forms. (3rd) DIPYLON or GEOMETRIC (B.C. 700), with fret pattern enrichment, and panels with rude figures of men and animals in black and brown. (4th) PHALERON WARE (B.C. 700-550), with continuous bands of animals, probably derived from Phœnicia or Assyria (fig. 4). Among the animals depicted, are placed portions of the fret pattern, a survival of the previous style. The details are incised through the black or brown figure, showing the colour of the clay body. A development of this Phaleron ware was the introduction of the rosette, taking the place of the fret pattern between the figures or the animals. (5th) BLACK FIGURE PERIOD (B.C. 600-480) vases, fine in profile, and with good handles, the body of the vase, in red ware, being painted with subjects of Grecian mythology in black, and the details incised; the faces, arms, and legs of the female figures were afterwards painted in white or red slip and fired at a lower heat. The AMPHORA (fig. 5) was the chief form of this black figure period—some fine examples are signed by Exekias and Amasis. (6th) The TRANSITIONAL PERIOD (B.C. 500-470), when the black silhouette figures on a red ground gave way to the RED FIGURE PERIOD on a black ground. Artists of this style were Epiktetos, Pamphæios, Nicosthenes, and Pythos. Many of the vases by Nicosthenes resemble contemporary metal work in their shape and handles. The 7th group (525-400 B.C.) was the culminating period of Greek vase painting, the chief form employed being the KYLIX. A fine series of these *Kylikes*, with red figures on a black ground, signed by Cachrylion, Euphronios, Duris, Pethenos, and Hieron, are in the British Museum.

The later vases (400-200 B.C.) are the polychrome sepulchral "Lekythi," covered with white slip, and enriched with paintings, and the elaborate vases, decorated with subjects from the Greek drama, which were produced in the Greek cities of southern Italy.

1 ROMAN: RED LUSTROUS, OR SAMIAN WARE: WITH ENRICHMENTS

2 IN RELIEF, OBTAINED BY PRESS-ING INTO MOULDS & BY THE USE OF DIES MUSEUM OF GEOLOGY.

3 ROMAN ORNAMENTED WITH PIPECLAY SLIP, ON BLACK GROUND. MUSEUM OF GEOLOGY

4 CHINESE VASE PAINTED WITH CHRYSANTHEMUMS & FOLIAGE in BLUE. MING DYNASTY. SOUTH KENSINGTON MUSEUM.

5 A PORTION OF OIRON POTTERY. INLAY OF COLOURED CLAYS, ON THE WHITE BODY OF THE WARE

6 CANDLESTICK. OIRON. OR "HENRI—DEUX" WARE. A.D. 1524–40. S.K.M.

7 JARDINIÈRE. ROUEN WARE 1720 A.D. S.K.M

8 PORCELAIN VASE SÈVRES. PERIOD OF LOUIS XVI S.K.M.

9 DISH OF SLIP WARE. BY THOMAS TOFT 1660. M OF G.

J.HOMASTOFT

10 WHITE, GREEN & LILAC JASPER. WEDGWOOD WARE. S.K.M.

11 MELEAGER. FULHAM STONEWARE BY DWIGHT. 1671–1700. BRITISH MUSEUM.

CERAMICS.

The antiquity of ceramic art and its scientific and artistic qualities, render this subject one of considerable interest to art students.

The plasticity of clay and its hardening qualities under the influence of intense heat, its adaptability to the most refined forms, its affinity for the beautiful glazes and enamels so often associated with pottery, and its splendid traditions of craftsmanship, of colour, form and decorations, so beautiful and varied in character, all combine to invest the subject with a charm or fascination of its own. Intrinsically valueless in its natural state, it is capable of being rendered almost priceless by scientific workmanship and artistic skill. The history of this material, and of its easy adaptation to the most refined and intricate, as well as the simplest of forms, affords invaluable lessons for present day students.

Pottery clay may be classified under three divisions or headings:—(1) EARTHENWARE, (2) STONEWARE, (3) PORCELAIN. Under the first are grouped the largest number of ceramic wares. The pottery of Egypt, the faience of Assyria and Persia, the Greek and Etruscan vases, the famous red ware from the Isle of Samoa, and its counterpart the Roman Samian ware, the beautiful Maiolica of Spain and Italy, and the Rouen, S. Porchaire, Delft, and most of our English pottery are earthenwares; the paste or body consists of natural clays selected for their plasticity, their hardening qualities, their fusibility or their colour, which when burnt have a porous opaque body, usually dull in colour. This dulness was usually overcome by coating the ware with a slip of fine white clay, which, whilst not possessing inherent qualities to form pottery by itself, would adhere to the coarser coloured body of the earthenware, thereby forming a smooth white ground. The early Greek vases of Naucratis, the later Lekythos of the Greeks, the faience of Persia, the Mezza Maiolica and the Sgraffito of the early Italian Renascence, and our English slip ware are examples of this method of giving a smooth white surface to coarse coloured earthenware. A similar result to the slip covering was also produced by the use of a silicious glaze, rendered white and opaque by the addition of oxide of tin. Early Assyrian faience, Della Robbia ware, the Maiolica of Spain and Italy, and the wares of Delft and Rouen are earthenwares coated with a tin enamel.

The silicious glaze here referred to is prepared by fusing silicious materials with soda or potash, and is known as Vitreous, or glass glaze. Plumbeous, or lead glaze, is produced by the addition of oxide of lead to the silicious glaze, rendering it more fusible, and still transparent. A white opaque enamel formed by using oxide of tin with the vitreous glaze, is termed Stanniferous, or tin enamel.

These different processes of covering the porous body of the earthenware largely influenced the decorations and scheme of colouring. The beautiful faience of Damascus and Rhodes is covered with the silicious slip or glaze, and painted with rich blues, produced by cobalt, turquoise and green, by cobalt and copper, and purple by the use of manganese, and then covered with an alkaline glaze.

In the Rhodian ware the same scheme of colour prevails, except that the purple is replaced by a fine opaque red of great body, called Rhodian red, produced from Armenian bole. On the Italian Maiolica, with its tin enamel and plumbeous glaze, there are fine blue, turquoise and green, but red is very poor in colour, and is generally replaced by rich yellow from antimony, and orange from iron. This white tin enamel was undoubtedly introduced into Europe by the Moors, as some tiles in the Alhambra date from 1273-1302.

A large number of bowls and dishes, known as Samian ware, but now called *Terra Sigillata* (seal clay), of Roman importation have been found in England. The paste is usually of a fine sealing-wax red, with a good glaze. These bowls are enriched with a series of horizontal bands, containing the festoon, the scroll, birds, animals, and figures. The bands, or friezes, are often divided by the traditional egg and tongue moulding (fig. 1). Clay moulds, impressed with stamps, were made and then fired. The red paste having been pressed into the mould, the interior was smoothly turned in the lathe. A mould of this character was found at York in 1874, so it is possible that some of this ware was made in England, by Roman potters. Roman pottery has also been found at Castor, near Peterborough, doubtless made at the former place, kilns for firing having been found on the same site. This Castor ware is usually brown, with a black glaze, being ornamented with indented tool marks, and raised slip patterns of pipeclay (fig. 3). Many Roman dishes and vases of a dark grey colour, ornamented with incised lines and raised bosses of clay, have been found in the Upchurch Marshes in Kent. Little artistic pottery of the mediæval period, however, is known to exist. Early in the 13th century beautiful encaustic tiles were made for the great monasteries, abbeys, and cathedrals.

About 1500, the production of tiles was introduced into Holland, quantities of small blue and white ones, decorated with scriptural subjects being made at Delft, and thence exported to England for the lining of fireplaces, etc. Some fine painted tiles or *Azulejos* were made at Valencia about the 17th century.

In the 16th century, the porcelain of China was introduced into Europe by the Dutch and Portuguese traders, and much of the Delft and Rouen ware subsequently produced was in imitation of this oriental porcelain. "Delft" ware, which takes its name from the small town of that name in Holland, dates from A.D. 1500, and is a ceramic coated with stanniferous enamel, decorated with a full and liquid brush upon the absorbent enamel ground, and then glazed with a plumbeous glaze. Some of this Delft ware is very fine in quality, the cobalt blues under the glaze being remarkably soft and rich in colour. Early examples were decorated with historical subjects, often containing numerous figures, the middle period being notable for its imitation of Chinese porcelain, and the application of coloured enamels on coloured grounds. Vast quantities of this kind of ware were manufactured up to 1760, and exported to all parts of Europe. The production of Delft ware was first introduced into England at Lambeth by some Dutch potters in 1676, being subsequently extended to Fulham, Bristol, and Liverpool.

The use of stanniferous enamel was introduced into France by Girolama della Robbia, son of Andrea della Robbia, during the reign of Francis I., 1516, and enamelled ware similar to the later productions of Urbino was made at Nevers, where also was produced a fine ware decorated with Persian *motifs* in yellow and blue. At Rouen, also, a fine earthenware covered with a tin enamel was manufactured, the decorations consisting of the lambrequins or scallop pattern, symmetrical in arrangement, and converging to the centre of the plate or dish. The ornament was based upon Chinese examples, influenced by the contemporary woven fabrics of France. The decorations were usually in blue and with overglaze painting, *i.e.*, after the white enamel was fired, finer and more delicate detail being obtained by this process, but at the cost of the purity and liquid softness of colour which is so characteristic of Delft and oriental underglaze painting.

In Rouen ware, the ground is generally white, but some fine examples at South Kensington have a soft yellow ground, a rich Indian yellow being sometimes introduced with the blue decoration. It was under the directions of Louis Poterat (1673), that this most beautiful faience was perfected.

Bernard Palissy (1510-90), by repeated experiments discovered the stanniferous or tin enamel. His first productions were Jasper ware, warm and brilliant in colour, and richly enamelled. In the second period, rustic dishes, elaborately decorated with carefully modelled fishes, reptiles, and plants or natural foliage, covered with an enamel of great brilliancy and purity, were the chief productions. The later pottery of Palissy consisted of saltcellars, inkstands, ewers, etc., the elaborate figure decorations of which were probably executed by some contemporary artist.

Henri-Deux or S. Porchard's ware, now more properly described as Oiron ware, originated at S. Porchard in 1524, perhaps by the hand, certainly under the patronage of Hélène de Hangest, widow of A. Gouffier, a former governor under Francis I. This Oiron ware, of a pale straw colour, is enriched with inlays of yellow, blue, green, and brown coloured pastes, the interlacing and arabesque ornamentation, carried out under the direction of Jehan Bernart and François Charpentier, being similar in type to the contemporary bookbinding of Grolier which was probably executed with similar tools.

Many early examples of Staffordshire slip ware are to be found in England, consisting chiefly of candlesticks, cups, tygs, posset pots, piggins and plates, the slip decorations being in yellow, white, and brown. This ware was made at Wrotham as early as 1649, and by Thomas Toft, at Shilton, 1660 (fig. 9). Marbled, combed, and tortoise-shell ware were formed by using colour slips or clays. Agate and onyx ware were formed by layers of different coloured clays, crossed, cut, and pressed into moulds. These methods were perfected by Thomas Wheildon (1740-98), and Josiah Wedgwood (1730-95), who perfected both the Queen's and the variegated ware. Queen's ware of a creamy colour was made chiefly for dinner and dessert services, being decorated with painted flowers in enamel.

In 1781, Wedgwood introduced his famous Jasper ware, and Jasper dip or washed Jasper. This latter ware was dipped into admixtures of metallic oxides, producing blue, lilac, pink, sage green, olive, yellow, and black as desired. The decorations in low relief are of the purest white (fig. 10), and in the traditional classic style, the figures being arranged as cameo medallions, or in bands with the scroll, the festoon, and the vine in delicate relief. Many of these beautiful cameos were designed or modelled by Flaxman (1755-1826), Pacetti and Angelini (1787), Bacon (1740-99), Hackwood (1770), Roubiliac (1695-1762), Stothard (1755-1834), Tassie (1735-99), and Webber (1782).

STONEWARE differs from earthenware, owing to the presence of a larger percentage of silicia in the plastic material, which, being fired at a greater degree of heat, vitrifies the body or paste into a kind of glass, thus ensuring a closeness and hardness of material not possessed by ordinary earthenware. Stoneware is usually glazed during the firing by throwing common salt into the kiln, which being volatilised, re-acts upon the silicia in the body, forming with it a silicate of soda or glass, having a minute granular texture. The usefulness and the artistic character of stoneware was perfected by the Flemish and German potters of the 16th century.

The principal varieties of this ware are the grey and white "Canette" of Siegburg, near Bonn, and the pale brown or grey ware of Raeren, near Aix-la-Chapelle, with its incised and stamped enrichments, sometimes with blue decoration. Frechen, near Cologne, probably supplied the "Bellarmines" or "Grey beards," largely imported into England under the name of "Cologne Pots." Examples of this Frechen ware were frequently ornamented with a raised scroll of oak leaves. Grenzhausen, in Nassau, produced a beautiful grey ware, having delicately moulded reliefs filled in with blue and purple. Many grey jugs ornamented with the initials of William III., Queen Anne, and George I., were imported into England from the Nassau kilns.

A peculiar kind of stoneware, also termed "Cologne ware" was produced at Fulham by John Dwight, about 1670. Some fine jugs and a few cleverly modelled unglazed statuettes, believed to have been made at this place, are to be seen in the British Museum (fig. 11).

Another peculiar red stoneware, porcelain, or Red China as it was called, was made near Burslem by the brothers Elers (1688-1710), the ornamentation being obtained by pressing sharp intaglio copper moulds upon pieces of clay attached to the shaped ware. Fine examples, characterised by beauty of outline and delicacy of enrichments, are exhibited in the Museum of Geology, Jermyn Street. Astbury (1710-39), continued the traditions of Elers, producing a fine white stoneware, which largely influenced the Staffordshire pottery of that period. A stoneware was also made at Nottingham from 1700-1750.

PORCELAIN is technically known under the terms "hard paste" ("pâte dure") and "soft" ("pâte tendre"). Hard porcelain is made from clays containing much aluminia and felspar or decomposed granite, having but little plasticity, which necessarily influenced the shape or profile of the vessel. The beauty of form which is so typical of the Greek earthenware vase, is absent in porcelain, where the cylindrical or octagonal form is principally used. "Pâte tendre" is a soft and vitreous porcelain, having a great affinity for the beautiful coloured glazes and enamels used in the early examples of Sèvres.

Porcelain was known in China about 200 B.C., and it was in common use during the 16th century. During the Ming dynasty (1568-1640), porcelain reached its highest development in the perfection of its body, ornamentation, colour and glazes, blue and turquoise being the chief colours of this period; this limited range of colour was owing to the intense heat required to fuse the felspar glaze upon the hard porcelain.

It is uncertain at what date Chinese porcelain was first brought to Europe. Amongst the earliest known pieces in England are some bowls given by Philip of Austria to Sir Thomas Trenchard in 1506. But whatever the date, it was inevitable that attempts should be made to imitate this beautiful ceramic. Florentine or Medician porcelain was made 1575-80. It was not, however, until 1690 or 1700, that a similar manufacture was established at Rouen and S. Cloud. In 1709, Bottcher commenced making hard porcelain at Meissen, in Saxony, subsequently producing some excellent examples about 1715. This was the commencement of the well-known Dresden china. In 1768, the manufacture of hard porcelain was adopted at Sèvres, replacing that of "pâte tendre" which had been in use from 1670. Both "pâtre dure" and "pâte tendre" were made at Buen Retiro in Madrid (A.D. 1759,) all the porcelain manufactured for the first twenty years being kept for the exclusive use of the Royal family. There are some finely modelled Buen Retiro tiles in the Royal Palace at Madrid.

About the year 1740, the manufacture of porcelain was established at Bow, Chelsea, Derby, Plymouth, Bristol, and Worcester. The shapes and ornamentation of these English porcelains, having no traditions beyond the oriental influence, were of a low artistic order, being simply copies of natural forms, without any controlling influence as regards design or harmonious arrangements. A lavish use of gilding was also characteristic of this period, the ornament being very largely misapplied. This continued to grow worse until the middle of the last century, when it reached its culminating point of absurdity and extravagance of form and decorations. The best examples of English porcelain of this period are obviously copies of oriental porcelain, chiefly Persian and Chinese. A great advance in the technique of the porcelain produced in this country took place after the discovery of Kaolin in Cornwall, by William Cookworthy (1755).

Transfer printing over the glaze was adopted at Worcester about 1757, the transfers being taken from copper plates engraved by Robert Hancock, a pupil of Ravenet, who was employed at the Battersea enamel works, about 1750. Sadler and Green in 1756 also adopted over glaze printing on the Liverpool delft. About 1770 under-glaze printing on the biscuit ware superseded the over-glaze process.

Of early English porcelains, those of Derby are, perhaps, the most refined in form and in treatment of decoration, the plates, cups, and saucers having borders of blue or turquoise, with enrichments of festoons, leaves, and flowers ; many of the cups were pressed with fluted, ribbed, or imbricated patterns. The Derby works were founded in 1757 by William Duesbury, who in 1769 purchased the Chelsea works and carried on the two simultaneously until 1784, when the Chelsea plant was transferred to Derby. From 1769-73 the ware called " Chelsea Derby " was produced, and between 1773-82 " Crown Derby" was introduced.

Porcelain of an excellent quality was made at Nantgarw about 1813, and at Swansea 1814-17, the decorations in enamel colours consisting of a natural rendering of flowers, birds, butterflies, and shells, chiefly painted by Richard Billingsley.

Porcelain was also made about 1800 at the Herculaneum potteries at Liverpool. Rockingham, in Yorkshire, produced during the years 1759-88 a brown china, which, however, was but a fine earthenware, of a hard and compact body, covered with a rich brown or chocolate glaze. In 1820, porcelain was made at Rockingham comprising dinner and dessert services, richly enamelled and gilt, together with vases, flower baskets, and busts in white biscuit ware. In 1832, a dessert service of 200 pieces was made for William IV., at a cost of £5,000, the decorations consisting of natural fruit and flowers, with landscapes and the royal arms in enamel colours.

In some of the earlier Rockingham ware the outlines of the flowers and butterflies were in transfer printing, and the colouring was added by hand.

The illustrations given on plates 28, 29, 35, 36, and 37 show the

universality of the potter's art, which may be traced through man
beautiful examples differentiated by racial customs and material.

The beauty of form in the Greek vase (plate 34), was but the
natural outcome of a fine earthenware in the hands of an artistic
people, with traditions and architecture of the highest order. In
Persian pottery, form is subservient to colour, blue, turquoise, and
white being used in charming combination, together with a frank yet
decorative treatment of natural forms.

The Hispano-Moresque and Italian Maiolica (plate 37), are
remarkable for the technical excellence of their white enamel, rich
blue, yellow, and orange, the iridescence of their gold and ruby lustre,
and their high technical skill in painting.

English earthenware of the 17th and 18th centuries, though traditional, showed a remarkable diversity in treatment and conception.
The picturesque platter of the Toft school, with its quaint enrichment
of trailing lines and heraldic forms in coloured slip, the fine red stoneware of Elers, with its graceful enrichments in delicate relief, and the
varied and beautiful jasper ware of Wedgwood mark a distinct phase
of the potter's art, and bear a tribute to the vitality and personality
of the founders of the " *Potteries*."

PAINTED
POTTERY.
14ᵗᴴ CENTURY
PERUVIAN.

SMITHIES
COLLECTION.

SALTING COLLECTION. S.K.M.

1

BLUE GROUND. ORNAMENT BUFF & ORANGE. CAFFAGGIOLO WARE 1500

2

HISPANO-MORESQUE. VALENCE 15TH CENTURY BLUE INSCRIPTIONS, WITH GOLDEN LUSTRED ORNAMENT.

3

PORTION OF BORDER OF A MAIOLICA PLATE ITALIAN 1550. INCISED OR SCRAFFIATO ORNAMENT. S.K.M.

4

PLATEAU FOR AN EWER BLUE ARABESQUES, ON ORANGE GROUND FAENZA. 1500 S.K.M.

5

A PILGRIM'S BOTTLE, BY ORAZIO FONTANA. URBINO WARE 1530. S.K.M

6

DRUG POT PAINTED IN GRISAILLE CASTEL DURANTE 1556 S.K.M.

7

BOWL GUBBIO WARE BY MAESTRO GIORGIO. 1501 S.K.M.

8

BOWL GUBBIO WARE. BY MAESTRO GIORGIO. S.K.M.

9

VASE BY MAESTRO GIORGIO. GOLD & RUBY LUSTRE. S.K.M.

10

VASE 1530 CASTEL DURANTE WARE. S.K.M.

MAIOLICA.

Maiolica or Italian faience is an earthenware, coated with a stanniferous or tin glaze, termed enamel. This is formed by the addition of oxide of tin to a silicious glaze or slip, thus rendering it white and opaque, hence its name, enamel.

The origin of this beautiful ceramic art may be traced to Chaldea and Persia, with their magnificent enamelled bricks, such as the " Frieze of Archers " from the Palace of Susa (455 B.C.), and now in the Louvre. From Persia the art was carried by the Arabians to Fustat, or old Cairo, which was destroyed A.D. 1168, and amongst the ruins many fragments of gold or copper lustred ware have been found. This enamelled ware was introduced into Spain in the 13th century, and perfected there by the Moors, giving rise to the Hispano-Moresque ware. This ware was enriched with central heraldic arms, surrounded by concentric bands of foliage, arabesques, or inscriptions in blue, with a copper lustre. This Hispano-Moresque ware was manufactured chiefly at Malaga, Talavera, Triana, and Valencia, and dates from the Moorish occupation of Granada (A.D. 1235-1492).

In the Island of Majorca, from which this beautiful ware derives its name, fine examples were manufactured at an early date by Persian and Arabian potters. After the conquest of Majorca by the Pisans (A.D. 1115), many of these examples were introduced into Italy, the art being subsequently cultivated in some of the smaller central states.

The early Italian Maiolica was usually covered with a thin white " slip " or engobe of clay, which served as a ground for the coloured patterns. It was then coated with a lead glaze, and was known as mezza or mixed Maiolica. In some examples the design was scratched or engraved through the upper layer or white engobe, showing the darker body underneath. This type of ware, known as *sgraffito*, was also glazed with the lead glaze, forming, when fired, the beautiful iridescent lustre.

Few remains of a tin enamel of Italian workmanship have been found in Italy prior to the time of Luca della Robbia (1400-1481), who discovered an enamel of peculiar whiteness and excellence. The secret of its composition was kept by him, his nephew Andrea, and his great-nephews Giovanni, Lucca, and Girolamo, until 1507. The mezza Maiolica was then superseded by the true Maiolica, or the tin enamelled wares of Caffaggiolo, Castel Durante, Urbino, Pesaro, Faenza, Forli, Diruta, Siena, and Gubbio—cities all within a limited district, lying towards the east coast of Italy, and renowned centres of the Maiolica fabrication.

The Gubbio ware is noted for its metallic ruby and golden lustre, and was signed by Maestro Georgio (Georgio Andreoli, 1518-1537):

the finest period of this master was about 1525. The same artist also lustred many wares made by the potters of Urbino and Castel Durante. Other examples of Urbino ware are signed by Niccola da Urbino (1490-1530); Orazio Fontana, the head of a noted family of potters, consisting of father, son, and grandson (1510-1600); Francesco Xanto Avelli (1530-40). Faenza ware was produced at the Casa Pirota Botega, and Siena ware was signed by Maestro Benedetto.

The chief characteristics of Caffaggiolo ware are arabesques and figures in white, grey, or yellow on a rich dark-blue ground. Urbino has small medallions with figures and blue and yellow arabesques on a white ground, called Raffaelesque, being from designs by Raffaelle del Colle. Faenza has a yellow ground with blue arabesques.

In brief, the number of colours that could be used on the absorbent tin enamelled ground with its lead glaze was somewhat limited, consisting of blue, turquoise, yellow, and orange. These colours are of great depth and translucency, and are only equalled by the blues and turquoise of China, Persia, and India.

Gubbio ware is frequently enriched with a raised curved fluting called *gadroons*, a most effective method of enhancing the beautiful ruby lustre of Maestro Giorgio. This Gubbio tradition was continued by Giorgio's son, Vicentio, called Maestro Cencio, and many beautiful lustre works are signed by him.

This lustre was produced by exposing the ware to the action of smoke during the firing in the kiln; the smoke, being carbon in a highly-divided state, reduces the metallic salts of the pigment or glaze, forming a thin film of metal upon the surface, the beautiful iridescent lustre resulting from the relative thickness of the film.

Castel Durante was frequently enriched, on white or grey borders, with delicate raised scroll-work in white slip or enamel, a process called *Lavoro di sopra bianco* or *bianco sopra bianco*.

Faenza Maiolica has, frequently, the whole surface of the ground covered with a dark-blue enamel, enriched with dancing amorini and arabesques in blue, heightened with white *Sopra Azzurro*.

A frequent form of enrichment upon plates was to have small medallions painted with portraits and appropriate inscriptions, and doubtless intended as lovers' presents. They are known as *Amatorii Maiolica.*

TERRA COTTA.

Terra cotta is usually made from pure clay, which will burn to a white or yellow colour, or from impure, which will burn to a red colour owing to the presence of oxide of iron. Pure clay is a hydrous silicate of alumina, containing 47 parts per cent. of silica, 40 of alumina, and 13 of water. Clay in this proportion is the Kaoline or china clay.

Fire clay, which is found in the coal measures, has a larger proportion of silica than Kaoline, and from it much of the terra cotta is made. When first dug out, it is hard and compact, and of a greenish-grey colour, deepening to black. It is often weathered before using; this causes it to "fall," and facilitates grinding. Old fire-clay, previously burnt ("grog" as it is called), is added to the new clay to counteract the excessive shrinkage to which all close-grained clays are liable.

The coarser the clay, the less the shrinkage. Pure clay contracts as much as one-eighth from the size of the mould: one-half of this contraction takes place in drying, the other half in burning.

The colour of the clay varies according to the quantity of lime, iron, or bitumen it contains.

The moulds for terra cotta are usually piece-moulds, made of plaster of Paris, which absorbs much of the moisture of the clay. Sheet clay about two inches thick is used. This is carefully pressed into the mould, and supported by webs of clay of the same thickness. It is essential that the clay be uniform throughout, or the shrinkage would be unequal. It is then placed upon a flue to dry, for from two to six hours, when the clay will have contracted sufficiently to allow the mould to be taken off. It is then dried for a further period, and burnt in a kiln. For fine work, the kiln is "muffled"—the "muffle" being a lining of bricks to keep the clay from actual contact with fire and smoke. The dry or semi-dry process is the pressing of clay-powder into metal moulds, which obviates the excessive shrinkage of the wet process. Encaustic tiles

GREEK TERRA COTTA. SELENE & PAN.

107

are made in this way, the ornament being run into the incised pattern with "slip." Many tiles are decorated in the same way as ordinary earthenware, that is, painted and glazed.

Terra cotta was largely used by the nations of antiquity, especially by the Assyrians, whose clay tablets or books throw so much light upon Assyrian history. With the Greek, terra cotta was extensively used for "antefixæ," and the many beautiful Tanagra figures now treasured in our museums show the exquisite modelling by the Greeks, in such a material as terra cotta.

GREEK
TERRA-COTTA

This material was used by the Etruscans for their sarcophagi and recumbent figures. The Pompeians tiled their roofs with terra cotta. It was used for votive statues and offerings, and for lamps, some of which were dipped in molten glass.

During the revival of art in Italy in the 15th and 16th centuries, terra cotta was extensively used by the Della Robbia family. Luca della Robbia (1400-82) produced many beautiful terra cotta reliefs, coated with the white tin enamel, and enriched with coloured enamels. Among his numerous works was the marble "Cantoria" or Singing Gallery (1431-40), with

A BAMBINO BY LUCCA & ANDREA DELLA ROBBIA

its ten panels of singing and dancing figures in relief, which was placed by the organ of S. Maria del Fiore, or Cathedral of Florence. Donatello's "Cantoria" was also placed here (page 57). They are now both in the museum of the Opera del Duomo. Lucca also executed five marble reliefs, in 1437, for the Campanile, from designs by Giotto, and the two kneeling angels holding candelabra, in the Sacristy of the Cathedral, Florence, are the only figures in the round by this master.

Among his many beautiful examples of terra cotta are the "Resurrection" and the "Ascension," over the doors of the Sacristy

108

in the Cathedral; the splendid monument to Bishop Federighi, with its beautiful recumbent figure of marble, in the Church of S. Trinita, Florence; the Tabernacle of Peretola; the Madonna of Or San Michele; and the many fine heraldic medallions, with the arms or emblems of the various Guilds, that enrich this beautiful Oratory of Florence (see page 58).

Other heraldic medallions in Florence are the Pazzi and Serristori arms for the Quaratesi Palace, and in the South Kensington Museum are some fine medallions with the arms of King Renè d'Anjou, and twelve medallions representing the months. Most of these examples have the typical quattrocento borders of fruit, flowers, and foliage or fir-cones (fig. 8, plate 21), and are enamelled in brilliant colours.

Ottaviano and Agostino Duccio, contemporary sculptors of repute, also collaborated with Lucca in the production of this ware. Andrea della Robbia (1435-1525), the nephew of Luca, carried on the traditions with rare selective power and artistic skill. Among his early works are the medallions with the *bambini*, for the Loggia of the Spedale degli Innocenti, or Foundling Hospital, at Florence, in collaboration with his uncle, Lucca, and Brunelleschi, the architect. The Adoration and the Annunciation were familiar subjects with Andrea. There is a splendid "Adoration" in the South Kensington Museum.

TERRA COTTA
RELIEF BY
ANDREA DELLA ROBBIA

STIBIUM CASE. ALABASTRON.
EGYPTIAN

GREEK OR PHŒNICIAN.
BRITISH MUSEUM

WITH A SPIRAL
THREAD IN BLUE.

AMPHORA.

AMPHORA

ROMAN TABLET IN RELIEF
WHITE CAMEO ON BLUE GROUND
MADE IN A MOULD. S.K.M.

THE PORTLAND VASE
BODY OF DARK BLUE GLASS.
THE FIGURES IN WHITE
BRITISH MUSEUM

ARABIAN ENAMELLED.
LAMP. S.K.M.

VENETIAN
16TH CENTURY

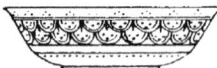

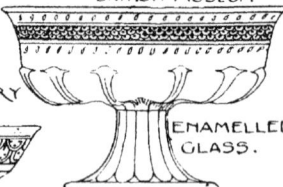

ENAMELLED
GLASS.

SOUTH KENSINGTON MUSEUM

VENETIAN
ENAMELLED CUP.

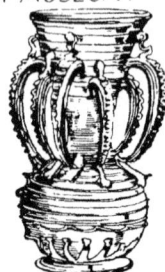

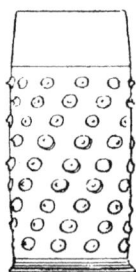

VITRO DI TRINA OR RETICULATED GLASS.

BRITISH MUSEUM

SPANISH CUP.

GERMAN.

GLASS.

The purity of glass, its adaptability to colour, and its remarkable ductility while hot for blowing, twisting, or drawing into threads, differentiates it from all other materials and methods of treatment. Its tradition dates from the remote past, for glass-blowing is represented on the tombs at Thebes (B.C. 2500). It was also used in Egypt for vitreous pastes for bronze and gold cloisonné jewellery, and for the small bottles or Stibium, with chevron patterns, in yellow, turquoise, and white on a coloured ground. Similar patterns, colours, and forms were used by Phœnicia and her colonies. Many remains of bowls were found in Assyria, one of transparent green glass having the name of Sargon (B.C. 722). Greece seems to have imported most of her glass from Phœnicia, but the Romans carried on the tradition, producing fine MOSAIC or MILLEFIORI. This was made by fusing rods of white and coloured glass together, then drawing it out to fine threads, and slicing it transversely; the section is then placed in a mould and a bubble blown, uniting the mosaic, which is then blown into various shapes. The Romans also used the interlacing of white and coloured rods, called LATICINIO, but they excelled in the CAMEO GLASS, of which the Portland vase is the finest known example. This vase is of dark blue glass, covered with white opaque glass, which was ground away with the wheel, leaving the figures in delicate relief. It was found in 1644 in the sarcophagus of Alexander Severus (A.D. 325), the subject of its relief being the myth of Peleus and Thetis. Another Roman example of cameo glass in the British Museum is the Auldjo vase or Oinochoè, with beautiful reliefs of vine leaves. Frequently these reliefs were blown or pressed into moulds (fig. 6). The tradition then declined until the 14th century, when the Venetians in the Island of Murano perfected the art of glass-making.

The earliest examples of VENETIAN GLASS were massive, richly-gilt, and enamelled in colours. One fine example in the British Museum is signed by its maker, " Magister Aldrevandini." In the 15th and 16th centuries, the most delicate and beautiful blown glass was made, often uncoloured, and with enrichments of knots and wings in blown and shaped blue glass. The Venetians used with equal skill all the old methods of glass-making—the MILLEFIORI; the LATICINIO, or threads of opaque white enclosing pattern; RETICELLI, a network of white lines enclosing at the intersections a bubble of air; and the beautiful VITRO DI TRINA, filigree or lace glass, formed by canes or threads of white or coloured glass being placed in a mould, a bubble being then blown in, and the glass afterwards taken from the mould and blown or twisted to the shape required. The artistic bronze mirrors of ancient and mediæval times now give way to the glass mirrors of the Venetians (A.D. 1500).

EARLY GRISAILLE GLASS. SALISBURY CATHEDRAL

EARLY GOTHIC BORDER FROM BOURGES CATHEDRAL

DECORATED GLASS FROM ST MARY'S TRURO.

DECORATED GLASS FROM YORK MINSTER

13TH CENTURY MEDALLIAN GLASS. SAINT CHAPELLE. PARIS.

STAINED GLASS,

With its depth and translucency, owes its intrinsic qualities to metallic oxides, such as cobalt, giving fine blues, silver, pale and deep yellows, pink from iron and antimony, and ruby from gold and copper, which also yields fine greens. When these oxides are mixed with the glass in its fused state, it is termed " pot metal," but if the coloured oxides are applied to the surface of the glass only, it is termed " flashed " or " cased glass." Ruby, owing to its depth of colour, is usually cased glass. Fine blues are often flashed, and splendid effects are produced by flashing ruby over yellow or blue pot-metal glass. Cased glass is of the greatest value, owing to the variety of tint that can be produced on a single sheet of glass, and also because the colour may be removed by grinding or by the use of fluoric acid.

The rationale of the glass painter is :—(1) The scheme of composition and colour shown on a small scale ; (2) a full-sized cartoon in charcoal or monochrome, with all the details carefully drawn, and showing the lead lines and positions of the iron stanchions for strengthening the window ; (3) a tracing on cloth showing the lead lines only, called the cut line, on which are cut the selected pieces of glass ; (4) a tracing of the details from the cartoon, with brown enamel, on each piece of glass, the pieces after firing being then fixed in the leading, and kept together with H-shaped leads.

PORTION OF A "JESSE" WINDOW, CANTERBURY CATHEDRAL.

The brown enamel, which is used entirely for outline, detail, or shading, is a fusible glass in combination with opaque manganic or ferric oxide and tar oil. With this enamel, smear shading or stipple shading is worked. This may be removed as required, before firing, by means of a pointed stick or quill, so as to give the details of embroidery or of heraldic forms.

Silver stain (oxide of silver), introduced at the beginning of the

14th century, is largely used in stained glass, and usually on the back thereof. According to the different degrees of heat in the firing, a pale yellow or deep orange of great transparency is produced.

Coloured glass was made by the Egyptians 4,000 years ago, but the earliest stained glass windows recorded were those at Brionde (A.D. 525). None, however, are known to be still in existence prior to those of S. Denis (A.D. 1108). The early examples found in Norman windows have small medallions of figures and ornament of a decided Byzantine type, extremely deep in colour, being, by their style of treatment, termed mosaic glass. The 13th century, or early Gothic period, has single lancet lights, with medallions containing small figures surrounded by the typical 13th century foliage; or the windows were entirely of ornament in *grisaille*, arranged symmetrically—or with a flowing treatment of the vine growing from the recumbent figure of Jesse, and called the " Tree of Jesse "— with narrow bands of ruby or blue, and wide borders. These *grisaille* windows are of a greenish-white glass, with the ornament in

EARLY GRISAILLE GLASS, SALISBURY.

outline, and the ground hatched with brown enamel in fine cross lines (figs. 1 and 2). The north transept window at York Cathedral, called the " Five Sisters," is typical of this *grisaille* glass. The finest examples, however, are at Salisbury, Canterbury, and Chartres Cathedrals. Later in the period, single figures were introduced under a simple canopy or gable, plain or crocketed, with an ordinary trefoil arch.

" Quarry " glass, square or diamond in shape, with brown enamel details, was frequently used where simple masses were desired.

"QUARRIES,"
ENGLISH
EARLY 16TH
CENTURY.
(S.K.M.)

In the 14th century, the figures were larger and placed under canopies in each light of the mullioned windows; such figures in rich colours form a bright belt across the window, surmounted by the canopies, cusped and crocketed, and in strong yellow pot metal, or yellow-cased glass. The borders were narrow, with a somewhat natural rendering of the rose, the maple, and the oak.

In the 15th century a further change took place, figures became more numerous, and the canopy or shrine larger, and chiefly in white glass, with the crockets and finials tipped with yellow stain : a good illustration is that given from All Saints' Church, York. The coloured border of the earlier glass is entirely absent, its place being taken by the shaft of the canopy, and the crockets, finials, and ornaments are square in treatment, and based chiefly on the vine leaf.

Fairford Church perhaps contains the finest series of late Gothic glass (A.D. 1500-30). Like the contemporary architecture of the 16th century, stained glass was now influenced by the Renascence. The canopy still survived, but was horizontal or pedimental in form, with purely classical columns and details. Good examples of this period are the windows of King's College Chapel, Cambridge (1520), where rich Renascence work is introduced into late Gothic mullioned windows. These windows are probably similar to those by Barnard Flower, glazier, placed in Henry the Seventh's Chapel at Westminster Abbey, as in Henry the Seventh's will it was expressly provided that " the walles, doores, windows, archies, and vaults and ymagies of the same, of our said chapell, within and without be painted, garnisshed, and adorned with our armes, bagies, cognoisaunts, and other convenient painteng, in so goodly and riche manner as suche a werk requireth, and to a King's werk apperteigneth " :—" that the windows of our said chapell be glased with stores [? stories], ymagies, armes, bagies, and cognoisaunts."

Of this glass little remains, but we know that a contract was made in the· time of Henry the Eighth to complete the windows of King's College Chapel, Cambridge, " with good, clene, sure, and perfyte glasse, and oryent colors and imagery of the story of the old lawe and of the new lawe, after the forme, maner, goodenes, curiousytie, and clenelynes, in every poynt of the glasse windowes of the Kynge's new Chapell at Westminster." This glasse was by Francis Williamson and Simon Symonds, glaziers, of London, and its cost was to be sixteen pence per foot. Galyen Hoone, Richard Bownde, Thomas Reve, and James Nicholson also agreed to execute eighteen windows of the upper story of King's College Chapel,

LATE GOTHIC WINDOW, NORTH AISLE, ALL SAINTS' CHURCH, YORK.

115

similar to those at Westminster by Barnard Flower, six of the windows to be set up within twelve months, and the bands of leads to be at the rate of twopence per foot.

At Warwick, the windows of the Beauchamp Chapel were glazed by John Pruddle, of Westminster, " with the best, cleanest, and strongest glasse of beyond the sea that may be had in England, and of the finest colours of blew, yellow, red, purpure, sanguine, and violet, and all other colours that shall be most necessary and best to make and embellish the matters, images, and stories that shall be delivered and appointed by the said executors by patterns in paper, afterwards to be traced and pictured by another painter, in rich colours, at the charges of the said glazier."

About 1540, transparent enamels were introduced with skill and reticence, but gradually glass painters began to vie with pictorial oil painting in effects of light and shade, the ground work or material losing that beautiful translucent or transmitted colour which is the chief glory of stained glass. An example showing the degradation of this art is the west window of New College, Oxford, painted by Jervas, in 1777, from designs by Sir Joshua Reynolds.

In the 14th century, the English craftsman attained a thorough mastery over his materials, and consequently the type of ornament followed English contemporary architecture more closely.

To sum up, stained glass changed through the different periods from the rich coloured mosaic of the Normans, the equally rich coloured medallions and *grisaille* glass of the early Gothic, the decorated Gothic, with glass in lighter colours and a prevalence of yellow stain, culminating in the later Gothic period, when largeness of mass, lightness, and silvery colour were the characteristics.

A beautiful treatment of stained glass, dating from the 15th century, was used by the Arabians. This glass, which has a singular gem-like quality and is without enamel or stain, was let into a framework of plaster, which had been cut and pierced with geometrical or floral patterns.

Modern stained glass has attained a high degree of perfection in design and material under Burne Jones, Walter Crane, Frederic Shields, and Henry Holiday, with glass such as that produced by Morris, Powell, and Sparrow, and the American opalescent glass of La Farge and Tiffany. The individuality of their work, appropriateness of treatment, based upon the splendid tradition of the past, mark a distinct epoch in the history of stained glass.

Splendid heraldic glass by A. W. Pugin may be seen in the Houses of Parliament, Westminster; and in the hall and staircase of the Rochdale Town Hall there is a fine series of windows by Heaton, Butler, and Bayne, remarkable for dignity of style and unity of conception.

ENAMELS.

Of the many decorative arts, enamelling is one of the most beautiful, having a singular charm of limpid or opalescent colour of great purity, richness and durability, and being capable of a most refined and varied treatment for the enrichment of metals.

Enamel is a vitreous or glass compound, translucent or opaque, owing its colouring properties to mineral oxides, or sulphides, a fine opaque white being produced by oxide of tin. These enamels require different degrees of heat in order to fuse them and to cause their adhesion to the metal. Enamels are divided into three classes :—CLOISONNE, CHAMPLEVE and PAINTED ENAMELS.

CLOISONNE enamel is that in which the cloisons or cells are formed by soldering thin, flat wire of metal upon a plate of copper, the cloisons being filled with the various enamels, in powder or in paste, then, in order to vitrify the enamel, it is heated in a kiln, if upon a flat surface, or by the aid of a blow-pipe if upon a curved surface.

Cloisonné was in use from the early dynasties in Egypt, many fine large pectorals having been found in the tombs. These usually have the form of a hawk and are of gold or bronze with well-defined cloisons, which were filled with carefully fitted coloured paste or glass, and this undoubtedly was the origin of the true or vitreous cloisonné enamel. Byzantine enamel is invariably cloisonné, and one of the most beautiful examples of this period is the Pala d'Oro of S. Mark's at Venice (A.D. 976, see page 123). Perhaps the Chinese and Japanese have carried this cloisonné to its greatest perfection in softness of colour and beauty of technique. The earliest Chinese cloisonné is of the Ming dynasty (1368-1643); this has heavy cast metal grounds with low toned colours and deep reds and blues. Under the Ch'ing dynasty, which commenced in 1643, the colours became brighter and the designs more refined.

Early Japanese cloisonné or " Shippo " was doubtless derived from Chinese or Persian sources, and it is characterised by extremely thin beaten copper grounds and the frequent use of a dark green ground in place of the dark blue of the Chinese cloisonné.

The Japanese cloisonné reached its culmination during the last century, when many splendid examples of refined and delicate enamels were produced, remarkable for their beautiful opalescent and translucent colour. Gold cloisons with opaque and translucent enamels were frequently inserted in iron or silver objects by the Japanese of this period.

An early example of English cloisonné is the jewel of King Alfred (page 121). A fine Celtic cloisonné treatment may be seen in the Ardagh chalice (page 121), where the cloisons were cut out of a plate of silver and embedded in the enamel while soft. The Celtic craftsmen also had a beautiful treatment of enamelling by engraving or

117

pressing a pattern in intaglio or sunk relief, on an enamelled ground, and then filling these intaglios with other enamels.

A most exquisite kind of enamel called "*Plique à Jour*" was used by the Byzantines : this was composed of open filigree cloisons, filled with translucent enamels.

CHAMPLEVE enamel is formed by engraving, casting or scooping out the cloisons from a metal plate, leaving a thin wall or boundary between each cloison, which is then filled with the various enamels as in the cloisonné method. This Champlevé method was practised in Britain before the Roman Conquest, and was probably derived from the Phœnicians, who, centuries before the Romans came to England, had traded with Cornwall for tin. The beauty of colour and perfect adaptability of these early enamelled brooches, fibulæ and trappings of horses of the early Britons and Celts, are remarkable, showing a fine sense of colour and a harmony of line and mass. A splendid bronze Celtic shield (fig. 6, plate 13), now in the British Museum, is enriched with fine bosses of red enamel. These Champlevé enamels upon bronze have usually an opalescent or cloudy appearance caused by the fusion of the tin in the bronze alloy during firing. Champlevé enamels were used with rare skill and refinement to enhance the beautiful art of the goldsmith during the Middle Ages ; the Chalice, the Paten, the Reliquary, the Thurible, the Crozier, and the bookcovers of the Churches, especially, were enriched with beautiful enamels. Classed among the Champlevé enamels is that method called JEWELLER'S ENAMEL or "*Baisse Taille*," in which the plate is engraved in low relief or beaten up in repoussé and then flooded with translucent enamel. The Lynn cup of the time of Richard II. is one of the oldest pieces of corporation plate and is covered with fine translucent blue and green enamels (plate 40).

In India, where fine colour is a splendid tradition, Champlevé enamel soon attained a remarkable perfection of technique and purity and brilliance of colour almost unknown to the Western nations. The Champlevé enamels of JAIPUR have most beautiful lustrous and transparent blues, greens and reds laid on a pure gold ground. PERTUBGHUR is renowned for the fine green or turquoise enamel fired upon a plate of gold ; while the enamel was still soft a plate of pierced gold was pressed into the enamel. This pierced plate was afterwards engraved with incidents of history or hunting. In RATAIN, in Central India, a similar enamel is made having a fine blue in place of the Pertubghur green.

The fine monumental brasses, of which many still remain in our English cathedrals and churches, are a survival of the Champlevé process, the cloisons, being usually filled with a black NIELLO, but occasionally the heraldic shields are enriched with coloured enamels. During the 11th and 12th centuries, LIMOGES was renowned for its Champlevé enamels, but early in the 15th century PAINTED ENAMELS were introduced and Limoges became the centre of this art, called late Limoges or GRISAILLE ENAMEL.

The enamel colours were now used as a pigment, and were painted and fired upon a copper plate. The enrichments in grisaille, or grey and white, were used upon a black, violet or dark blue ground, the grisaille afterwards being enriched with details of fine gold lines. These Limoges enamels have a splendid technique, but they lack the charms of the luminous colour and judicious use of enamels of the early Champlevé period. The most renowned masters of the painted enamels of Limoges were Penicand (1503), Courtois (1510), Pierre Raymond (1530-1570), and Leonard Limousin (1532-1574). About 1600-1650 Jean Toutin and his pupil Petitot produced some fine painted miniatures in opaque enamels upon gold, remarkable for delicacy and perfection of enamelling. In 1750 painted enamel was introduced into England and produced for about thirty years at Battersea by Janssen. The enrichment consisted of flowers painted in natural colours on a white ground. A similar enamel was also produced at Bilston in Staffordshire.

The finest enamels undoubtedly are those in which the enamel is used in small quantities, such as in the Celtic jewellery, the book-covers, and the Church and Corporation plate of the Gothic and early Renascence period, and the early Byzantine cloisonné, such as the Hamilton brooch in the British Museum, and the Pala d'Oro of S. Mark's, Venice, which was made at Constantinople for the Doge Orseolo in A.D. 976, and has 83 panels of fine cloisonné enamel set in a framework of gold.

The "*Plique à jour*," the "*Baisse taille*" and the Pertubghur enamels are fine examples of appropriateness of treatment with translucency or opalescence and richness of colour.

The Japanese cloisonné with its literal treatment of natural forms, and the painted enamel portraits of Francis I. and contemporary princes by Leonard Limousin, clever as they undoubtedly are, lack the depth and purity of colour obtained by the early methods. Frequently, however, the Penicauds, Nardou, and Jean I. and II. obtained some richness in the painted enamels by the use of "*Paillons*" or pieces of metallic foil which were afterwards flooded with translucent enamel.

ROMAN
SILVER CUPS,
FROM THE TREASURE-TROVE
OF HILDESHEIM, BERLIN.

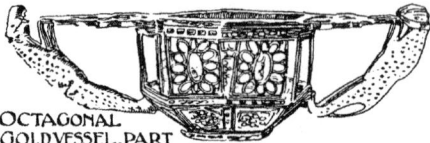

OCTAGONAL
GOLD VESSEL. PART
OF THE TREASURE OF PETROSSA.
BUKAREST MUSEUM.

THE TARA
BROOCH.
10TH CENTURY
DUBLIN.

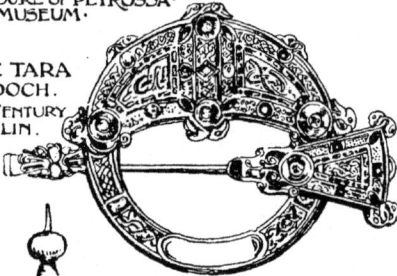

THE
LIMERICK
CROSIER.
SILVER GILT.
PASTORAL
STAFF,
ENRICHED WITH
TRANSLUCENT
ENAMELS.
IRISH.
EARLY
15TH CENTURY.

THE LYNN CUP
SILVER GILT
& ENAMELLED
ENGLISH
14TH CENTURY
CORPORATION OF
KINGS LYNN.

DESIGN FOR
QUEEN JANE
SEYMOURS
GOLD CUP
BY HOLBEIN
1536
BODLEIAN
LIBRARY,
OXFORD

OLD AND SILVER,

With their intrinsic value, ductility, and beauty of colour, have long been associated with the decorative arts of the past, and the many splendid examples still in existence are a tribute to the culture and personality of the craftsman.

Beautiful early examples were found in 1859 with the mummy of Queen Aah-Hotep (1800 B.C., Cairo Museum), and consisted of bracelets, armlets, rings, chains, a diadem, a small model of a war galley, and a poniard, all of exquisite workmanship and of pure gold, enriched with jasper and turquoise vitreous pastes. At Petrossa, in 1837 (Bukarest Museum), some splendid gold objects of Byzantine workmanship were found, consisting of two neck-rings or Torques, a large salver, hammered and chased, a ewer, a bowl with figures in repoussé, four fibulæ enriched with precious stones, a gorget, and two double-handled cups (plate 40). At Guarrazar, in Spain, ten gold votive crowns of Gothic workmanship were found: one inscribed with the name of King Suintila (A.D. 630) is now in the Museum at Madrid; the others are in the Hôtel Cluny, Paris, the largest having the name of King Rescesvinthus (A.D. 670) in pendive letters.

Of silversmiths' work, the most important is the "Treasure of Hildesheim," found in 1868 (Berlin Museum), consisting of thirty objects, cups, vases, and dishes, beautiful in contour and admirably enriched with delicate repoussé work of the Greco-Roman period (plate 40).

Of the gold and silver vessels used by Solomon in the temple, we have only a representation of the seven-branched golden candlestick on the Arch of Titus, at Rome.

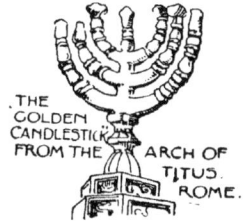

THE GOLDEN CANDLESTICK FROM THE ARCH OF TITUS. ROME.

English work of an early date is rare, but there are two very beautiful examples, one, the gold ring of Ethelwulf, enriched with blue Champlevé enamel, now in the British Museum, and Alfred's jewel of gold, with cloisonné, opaque, and translucent enamels, with the inscription "Alfred me has worked": this is, with the single exception of the S. Ambrose altar-frontal, the oldest signed enamel extant (871-901, Ashmolean Museum, Oxford).

SILVER BOWL with REPOUSSE PLAQUES OF GOLD

THE ARDAGH CHALICE IN THE ROYAL IRISH ACADEMY

Contemporary Irish work was even more skilful, and the Ardagh chalice of silver, with gold filigree and enamel enrichments, and the Tara brooch (plate 40) are fine examples.

The wealth and elaborate ritual of the mediæval church called

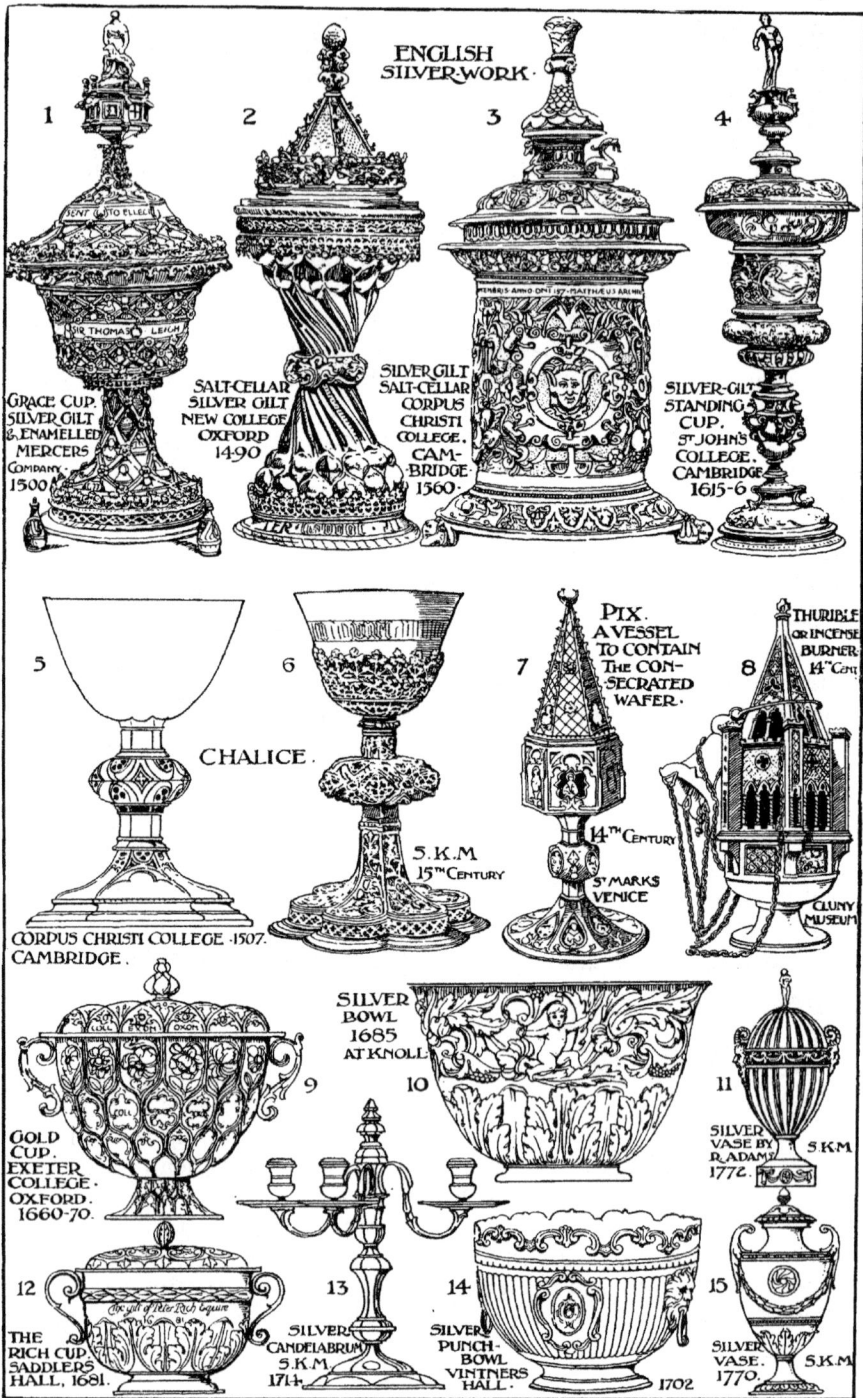

ENGLISH
SILVER·WORK·

1

2

3

4

GRACE·CUP.
SILVER·GILT
& ENAMELLED
MERCERS
Company·
1500·

SALT·CELLAR
SILVER·GILT
NEW·COLLEGE
OXFORD·
1490·

SILVER·GILT
SALT·CELLAR
CORPUS
CHRISTI
COLLEGE.
CAM-
BRIDGE·
1560·

SILVER·GILT
STANDING
CUP.
St·JOHN'S
COLLEGE·
CAMBRIDGE·
1615-6·

5

6

CHALICE·

7

PIX.
A·VESSEL
TO·CONTAIN
THE·CON-
SECRATED
WAFER·

8

THURIBLE
OR·INCENSE
BURNER·
14"·Cent·

5·K·M
15TH·CENTURY

14TH·CENTURY
S·MARKS
VENICE·

CLUNY
MUSEUM·

CORPUS·CHRISTI·COLLEGE·1507·
CAMBRIDGE·

9

SILVER
BOWL
1685
AT·KNOLL·

10

11

SILVER
VASE·BY
R·ADAMS
1772·

5·K·M

GOLD
CUP.
EXETER
COLLEGE·
OXFORD·
1660-70·

12

13

14

15

THE
RICH·CUP
SADDLERS
HALL·1681·

SILVER·
CANDELABRUM·
5·K·M·
1714·

SILVER
PUNCH-
BOWL
VINTNERS
HALL·

1702·

SILVER
VASE·
1770·

5·K·M

forth the finest effort of the craftsman, more especially the gold and silversmiths, who in England, perhaps more than in other countries, produced abundant examples of ecclesiastical plate. Altar-frontals of gold, used only on rare festivals, are some of the richest relics of the past. An early example (11th century) was given by the Emperor Henry II. to the Cathedral of Basle (Cluny Museum). It is of gold, 3 ft. high and 5 ft. 6 in. wide, and has many figures in relief. At S. Ambrose, Milan, is an altar-frontal of silver-gilt, set with precious stones and enamels, and signed by "Wolvinus," an Anglo-Saxon, and dated A.D. 838. The great altar-frontal or Pala d'Oro of S. Mark's, Venice, was commenced in 976 at Constantinople. It is 9 ft. 9 in. wide, and 6 ft. 6 in. high, consisting of 83 plaques of gold, on which are figures of our Saviour, angels, and saints in cloisonné enamels, and set with precious stones.

The early two-handled chalices were frequently very large, and it is recorded that Charlemagne gave one of pure gold, set with precious stones, and weighing 53 lbs., to S. Peter's at Rome. From the 12th century the chalice became smaller and without handles, and the bowl semi-ovid or conical. The knob or boss on the stem, together with the base, are usually lobed or hexafoil, and enriched with repoussé work and enamels (plate 41).

The pax, introduced in the 13th century, was a small rectangular plaque, used in the celebration of the Mass to convey the kiss of peace. The cross, the shrine, the reliquary, the pix, the ciborium, the monstrance, the thurible or censer were of gold and silver, enriched with jewels and enamels or delicate repoussé work.

The pastoral staff, or crosier, was first a staff of wood, capped by a ball or knob with a simple volute ; then later the knob developed into tabernacle work, with canopies and figures, and the volute or crook, enriched with crockets, frequently enclosed the *Agnus Dei* (Lamb of God) or other sacred group. The early crosiers (12th or 13th centuries) were usually of copper, gilt and enamelled, and of Limoges workmanship. From the 14th century, gold, silver, and ivory were the materials generally used, The Limerick Crosier is a good illustration of this period (plate 40).

Contemporary with this splendid ecclesiastical work was the college and corporation plate, of which the Lynn Cup (plate 40) is perhaps one of the most beautiful among many magnificent examples extant. The Leigh Cup (plate 41, fig. 1) and salt-cellar (fig. 2) are also of the Gothic period, but with the first half of the 16th century, the Renascence appears in the works of the great goldsmiths, such as Benvenuto Cellini, of Italy, Etienne de Laune, of France and Jamnitzer, of Germany. With Holbein's design for a gold cup (plate 40) the English Renascence appears, and civic plate was enriched with strap-work and cartouches, with foliated pendants of fruit and flowers (figs. 3 and 4, plate 41). In the 17th century, the acanthus foliage, with delicate chasing and relief, is the chief feature.

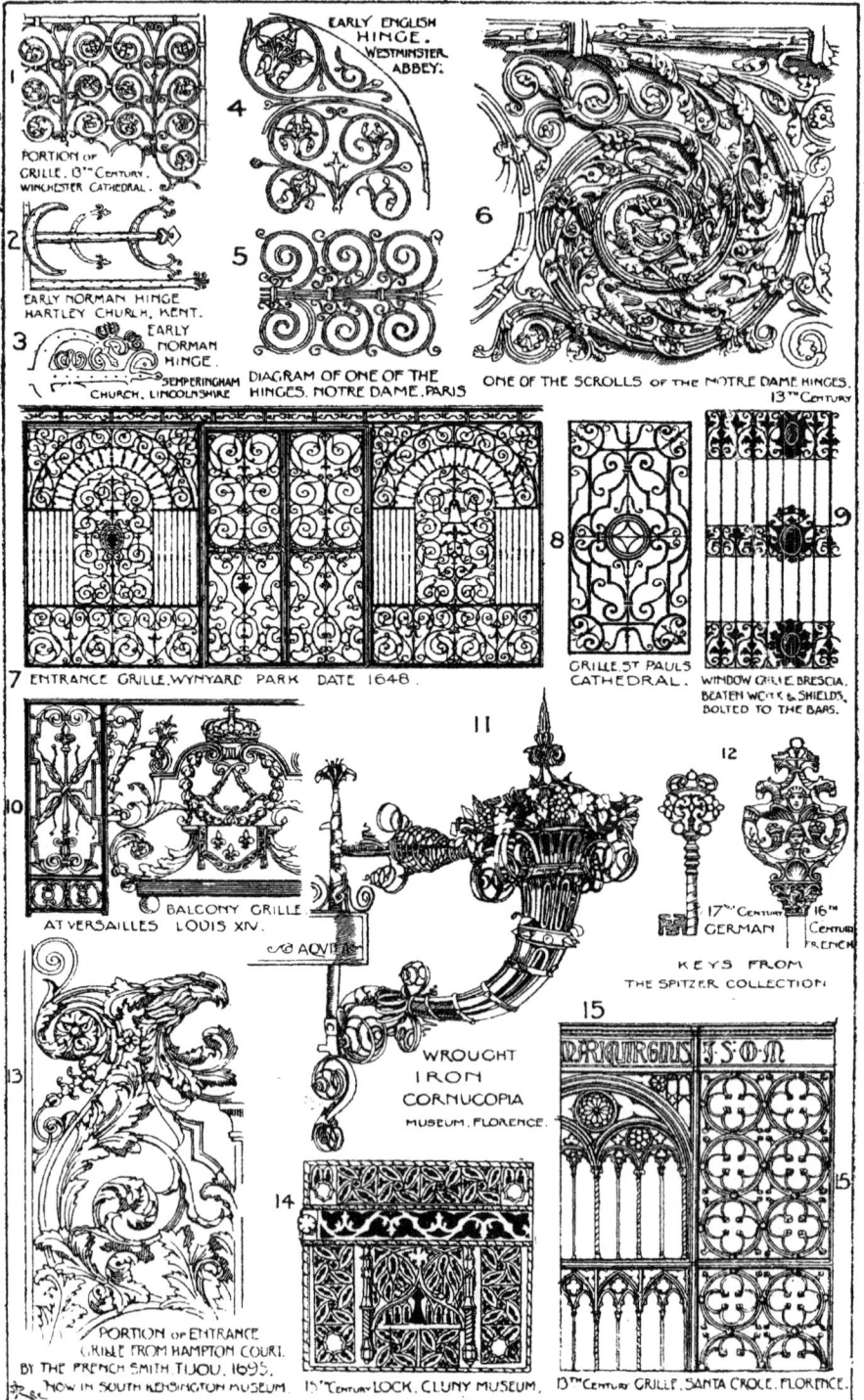

1 PORTION OF GRILLE. 13TH CENTURY. WINCHESTER CATHEDRAL.

2 EARLY NORMAN HINGE. HARTLEY CHURCH. KENT.

3 EARLY NORMAN HINGE. SEMPERINGHAM CHURCH. LINCOLNSHIRE

4 EARLY ENGLISH HINGE. WESTMINSTER ABBEY.

5 DIAGRAM OF ONE OF THE HINGES. NOTRE DAME. PARIS

6 ONE OF THE SCROLLS OF THE NOTRE DAME HINGES. 13TH CENTURY

7 ENTRANCE GRILLE. WYNYARD PARK DATE 1648.

8 GRILLE. ST PAULS CATHEDRAL.

9 WINDOW GRILLE. BRESCIA. BEATEN WORK & SHIELDS. BOLTED TO THE BARS.

10 BALCONY GRILLE AT VERSAILLES. LOUIS XIV.

11 WROUGHT IRON CORNUCOPIA. MUSEUM. FLORENCE.

12 17TH CENTURY GERMAN. 16TH CENTURY FRENCH. KEYS FROM THE SPITZER COLLECTION.

13 PORTION OF ENTRANCE GRILLE FROM HAMPTON COURT. BY THE FRENCH SMITH TIJOU. 1695. NOW IN SOUTH KENSINGTON MUSEUM.

14 15TH CENTURY LOCK. CLUNY MUSEUM.

15 13TH CENTURY GRILLE. SANTA CROCE. FLORENCE.

ROUGHT IRON.

The decorative qualities of iron, with its strength, durability, and comparative cheapness, have rendered it one of the most useful metals in the applied arts. Many fine Norman hinges of wrought iron are still in existence, having a straight central bar or strap, with small scroll terminations; these central straps were strengthened with crescent-shaped pieces, terminating in small serpent forms, probably a survival of the Viking traditions. This form of hinge was succeeded by the early Gothic hinge, which was a series of spirals springing from the straight bar or strap, the spiral being welded or fastened with collars; these spirals were enriched with a three-lobed foliage, or trefoil, typical of the early Gothic period; fine examples of this hinge occur on the west door of Notre Dame, Paris, where this typical spiral has the trefoil leaf, with birds, dragons, and small rosettes in stamped iron. This stamped characteristic may be seen, but in a less degree, in the fine hinges of Leighton Buzzard Church, Eaton Bray Church, Bedfordshire, and the Eleanor grill in Westminster Abbey, by Thomas de Leghton, in 1294. In the 14th and 15th centuries, when panelled doors took the place of the earlier doors, this early Gothic style of hinge was not needed (fig. 5), so that we find no trace of it in that period, but the art of wrought iron was continued with the hammered and chiselled hinges and lock plates of the most varied and delicate workmanship, which enriched the beautiful Gothic chests of the 14th and 15th centuries. The simple wrought screen, which was so largely used in the 13th century was now elaborated, especially in Italy, and fine examples of quatre-foil grilles with massive wrought framing and a rich frieze of foliage, cupids, and animals in pierced and hammered iron are to be seen at the cathedrals of Orvieto, Prato, and Siena, dating from about 1337 to 1350, and at Santa Croce, Florence (1371); but it was in Spain and France that the screen reached its culmination. The Spanish screens or "Réjas" in the cathedrals of Seville, Toledo, and Granada have a fine range of turned and chiselled vertical bars some 30 to 50 feet high, with an elaborate frieze and cresting.

Beautiful wrought and chiselled gates were erected in France about 1658, for the Louvre and Royal Chateaux of Anet and Econeu. There are some fine wrought gates at S. Paul's and at Hampton Court by Jean Tijon, who published some drawings of them in 1694, and many good simple gates of the last century are still in existence in many parts of the country.

The wrought iron gate piers in St. George's Chapel, Windsor, with their architectural treatment of open panelling, cresting, and massive buttresses, are filed, bolted and riveted, and are splendid examples of Flemish workmanship, probably by Quintin Matsys (1450-1529).

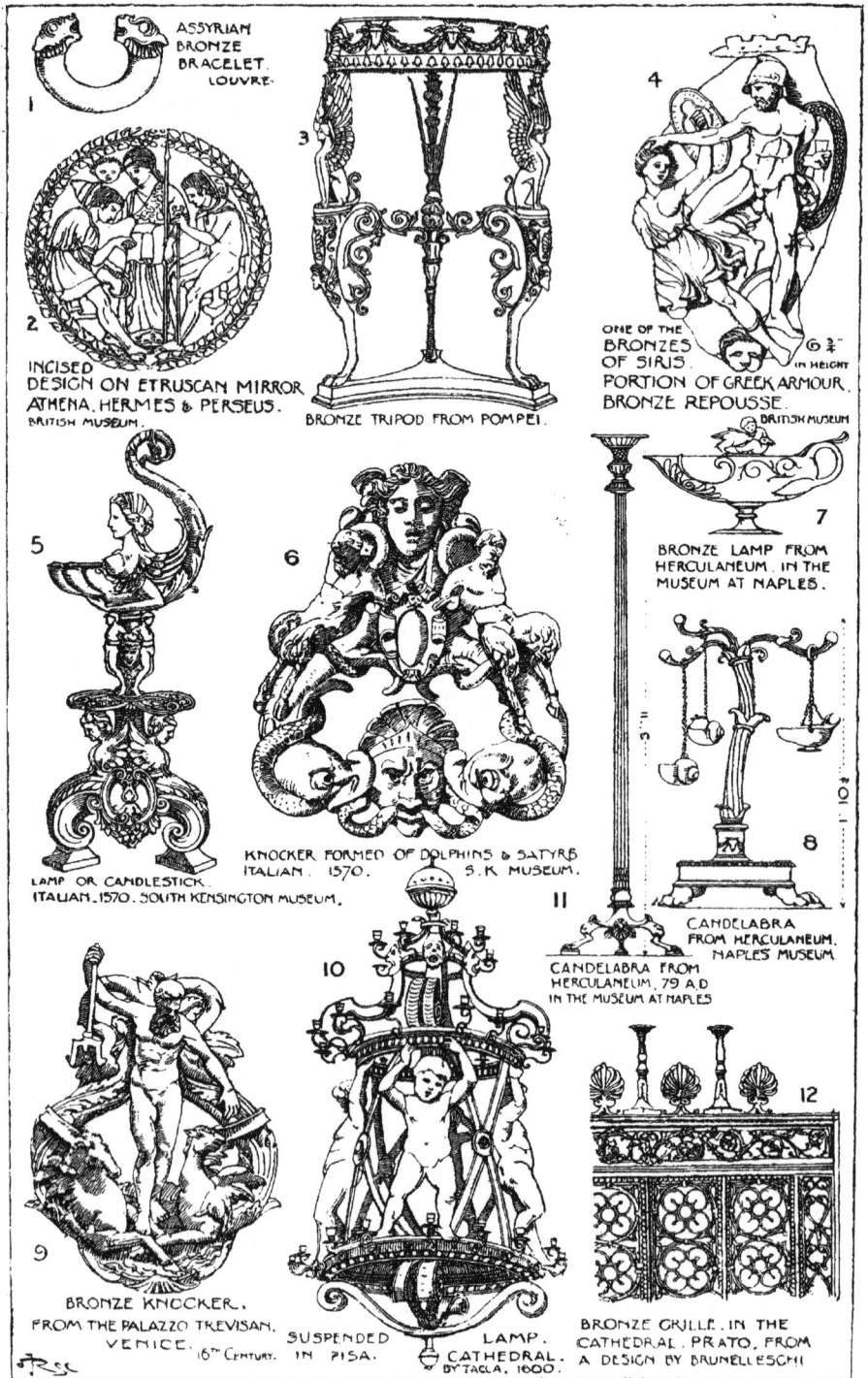

ASSYRIAN BRONZE BRACELET. LOUVRE.

1

2 INCISED DESIGN ON ETRUSCAN MIRROR ATHENA, HERMES & PERSEUS. BRITISH MUSEUM.

3 BRONZE TRIPOD FROM POMPEI.

4 ONE OF THE BRONZES OF SIRIS. IN HEIGHT PORTION OF GREEK ARMOUR. BRONZE REPOUSSE. BRITISH MUSEUM

5 LAMP OR CANDLESTICK. ITALIAN. 1570. SOUTH KENSINGTON MUSEUM.

6 KNOCKER FORMED OF DOLPHINS & SATYRS ITALIAN. 1570. S.K. MUSEUM.

7 BRONZE LAMP FROM HERCULANEUM. IN THE MUSEUM AT NAPLES.

8 CANDELABRA FROM HERCULANEUM. NAPLES MUSEUM

9 BRONZE KNOCKER. FROM THE PALAZZO TREVISAN. VENICE. 16TH CENTURY.

10 SUSPENDED LAMP. IN PISA. CATHEDRAL. BY TACLA. 1600.

11 CANDELABRA FROM HERCULANEUM. 79 A.D. IN THE MUSEUM AT NAPLES

12 BRONZE GRILLE. IN THE CATHEDRAL. PRATO. FROM A DESIGN BY BRUNELLESCHI

BRONZES.

Bronze, an alloy of copper and tin, has been in use from a remote period; its adaptability for casting, its durability and colour, render this material one of extreme beauty and usefulness. Among the many examples of antiquity are the 1,000 statues of Osiris, found in the temple of Rameses III., and the bands of figure subjects in relief from the Assyrian Balawat gates, now in the British Museum. In Greece, bronze was wrought with exquisite skill and refinement, and the name of Lysippos (340 B.C.), is usually associated with the finest statues.

Two beautiful repoussé bronzes (fig. 4), probably by Lysippos, found in 1820 near the river Siris, in Italy, are admirable examples of this period. Many Greek statues have been found in Pompeii and Herculaneum, of which the beautiful statuette of Narcissus is the best known, and many bronze heads are still extant with the eyes formed of ivory or beautiful stones and jewels.

Etruscan bronzes have a most expressive treatment of incised lines, which differentiates them from the repoussé work of the Greeks. The bronze mirrors with an incised treatment of classic mythology (fig. 2), and the cistæ, or toilet caskets, all found, with but few exceptions, at Palestrina, are typical of Etruscan bronzes. The finest example known is the " Ficoroni Cista " of the 3rd century, B.C. Its cylindrical sides are enriched with a representation of the " Argonauts," by Morios Plantios, and it is now in the " Collegio Romano " (see " Magazine of Art," 1880, and " Murray's Handbook of Greek Archæology"). Of small decorative bronzes, Naples museum alone has over 14,000 examples, consisting of candelabra, tripods (figs. 3, 7, 8, and 11), tables, chairs, and couches, which eighteen centuries ago were used by wealthy Roman citizens.

Early bronze equestrian statues are the " Nero " found at Pompeii (Naples museum), and the Marcus Aurelius at Rome (A.D. 175, plate 44). The four bronze horses, now in front of S. Mark's, at Venice, are probably of the time of Nero. Later examples are the " Gattamelata " at Padua, by Donatello (1453), the magnificent " Colleone " at Venice (plate 44), by Verrochio and Leopardi, and the " Louis XIV." by Girardon, cast by Jean Baltazar Keller in 1699, and destroyed in the French Revolution. Many fine bronze effigies are still extant, which replaced the earlier effigies of Purbeck marble, such as the Earl of Salisbury at Salisbury (1227), and the earliest recumbent figures in gilded bronze are those of Henry VI. (1272), and Queen Eleanor (1291), in Westminster Abbey, by William Torell, goldsmith of London. In Canterbury Cathedral is the fine effigy of the Black Prince (1376). The Richard II. and his Queen, in Westminster Abbey, are by Nicholas Broker and Geoffrey Prest (1395), and at Warwick is the magnificent Earl of Warwick, by William Austin and Thomas Stevens (1453).

127

EQUESTRIAN STATUE
OF BARTOLOMEO
COLEONE.
BY ANDREA
VERROCCHIO
& ALESSANDRO
LEOPARDO.
A.D. 1488.
VENICE.

EQUESTRIAN STATUE
OF MARCUS AURELIUS.
ROME. A.D. 175.

1554.

ONE GATE OF BAPTISTERY
AT FLORENCE, BY
LORENZO GHIBERTI.

STATUE OF PERSEUS
BY CELLINI.
FLORENCE.

The Florentine Torrigiano in 1512, made the beautiful recumbent effigies of Henry VII. and his Queen (see page 73), and also the Countess of Richmond, which are in Westminster Abbey, where there are also the gilded bronzes of the Duke of Buckingham (1628), and the Duke and Duchess of Richmond (1623), by an unknown artist. The statue of Charles I. by Le Sueur, and the Charles II. at Chelsea, and the James II. at Whitehall, by Grinling Gibbons, are later English examples of bronzes.

In Rome, the recumbent effigies of Sixtus IV. (1493), and Innocent VIII., which are the finest of Renascence bronzes, were by Antonio Pollajuolo. In 1508 Michel Angelo made the colossal seated statue of Pope Julius II., which was over the door of S. Petronio at Bologna. Benvenuto Cellini (1500-70), was the great Florentine goldsmith; his " Nymph of Fontainebleau," a relief in bronze for the lunette over the door of the Palace, is now in the Louvre, but his masterpiece is the " Perseus " (plate 44), in the Loggia dei Lanzi, at Florence, where the " Judith and Holofernes " by Donatello is also placed. Another eminent master was Giovanni da Bologna, who executed the beautiful fountain with the figure of Neptune, at Bologna.

The Shrine of S. Sebald at Nuremberg, by Peter Vischer (1508-9), and the figure of the Emperor Maximilian at Innsbruck, by Lodovico Scalza of Milan, which is enclosed by an elaborate grille, and surrounded by twenty-eight large bronze statues of men in armour, are excellent examples of German Renascence.

Many of the early historical buildings still retain their original bronze gates. Those of the Pantheon (A.D. 118-38), are still in position, also those of the cathedral at Hildesheim, with the panels of scriptural subjects in high relief, and the name and date of Bishop Bernward (1015). Early Byzantine gates cast in Constantinople by Staurachios, are at Amalfi (1066), and at S. Salvator, Atrani (1087), enriched with figures in silver damascening.

The west door of San Zeno, Verona (12th century), is of wood, covered with panels of repoussé work (see plates 1-3, "Arata Pentelici," by Ruskin). Early cast bronze gates in Italy are those of S. Ambroise, Milan (1170), and at Trani, Ravello, and Monreale Cathedral (by Bonanno, 1186), having relief panels and bosses upon the style of the door. In 1150, Bonanno cast some gates for the cathedral at Pisa, which were destroyed, with the exception of one, by fire in 1596, the west door being replaced in 1600 by a fine work by Giovanni da Bologna.

Of the Renascence bronzes, the Baptistry gates are the most remarkable (see page 44), while others are those of S. Peter's, by Simone and Filarete (1439), the door of the old Sacristy of the cathedral at Florence, by Lucca della Robbia (the only bronze by this master, 1464-74), and the " Baldacchino " of bronze, 95 ft. high, covering the high altar of S. Peter's, and cast from the ancient bronze enrichments of the dome of the Pantheon, by order of Pope Urban VIII., in 1633.

1 RENASCENCE TABLE. BARDINI COLLECTION   LATE 16TH CENTURY

2 BY DE CERCEAU

3 GRÆCO-ROMAN MARBLE TABLE. POMPEII.

TWO LATE RENASCENCE TABLES, CLUNY MUSEUM.

4   5

6 CARVED CASSONE, ITALIAN, 16TH CENTURY   SOUTH KENSINGTON MUSEUM

CORONATION CHAIR WESTMINSTER ABBEY. EDWARD I

RENASCENCE CHAIRS. CLUNY MUSEUM.

7   8   9   10

ECORATIVE FURNITURE.

Caskets, chests, and cabinets, chairs, tables, couches, and bedsteads have been of universal use during many ages, differentiated in design and craftsmanship according to the culture, wealth, and customs of the people, and the versatility, inventiveness, and skill of the craftsman. Many materials have been used for furniture, the chief being wood of various kinds, which was selected for its constructive qualities, beautiful texture, grain, and colour, and its adaptability to carving and inlay.

The universal use of the chair has doubtless tended to preserve its typical form through many centuries, and though undergoing various

EGYPTIAN CHAIR. FROM THE TOMB OF RAMESES III B.C 1200

2

3

OF WOOD. COVERED WITH GOLD & IVORY.

4

FROM A BAS-RELIEF   FROM A GREEK VASE.

CHAIR OF S^T PETER 1ST CENTURY

modifications, it has still retained its essential character as a seat. Numerous illustrations of early chairs are found on the carved reliefs of ancient Egypt and Assyria, and there are in the British Museum some early Egyptian chairs, one of which is of ebony, with uprights turned in the lathe, and inlaid with ivory. Many Greek chairs, remarkable for their simple and beautiful form, are shown upon the early Greek vases; and the Roman "Sella Curulis," or chair of senators and consuls, is represented on the Byzantine ivories (plate 46, fig. 9).

The Chair of S. Peter, of the 1st century A.D., which has enrichments of ivory and gold, is purely architectonic in form, and the same may be said of the coronation chair (fig. 7), which is the earliest example extant in England. The Gothic chairs, few of which remain, were of the box form, with carved linen-fold panels. During the age of Elizabeth, chairs were of oak, with turned supports, the back having an arcade in low relief or in open work. This form of chair was continued during the reign of James I., when the "Farthingale Chair" (chair without arms) was introduced. In the period of Charles I., walnut was introduced, and the chairs had twisted supports and rails, the back and seat being covered with pigskin

VENETIAN CHAIR 16TH Cent^y

131

or with stamped and coloured Spanish leather. In the reign of Charles II. and James II., the twisted or the carved and scrolled form of legs were common, with the seat and portion of back in cane, and the back, cresting, and rails in richly-carved open work, similar to fig. 10. In the time of William and Mary, the long supports were turned, and the front supports and arms turned and scrolled, the back of the chair being of open work, or covered with plain or patterned velvets. The chairs with simple curved or cabriole front legs, the arms, seat, and back upholstered with cut velvets, are characteristic of the Queen Anne period.

With George II. and III., we come to the use of mahogany and the work of Thomas Chippendale, who published a work on furniture in 1754, 1759, and 1762. His chairs have frequently straight legs, with shallow sunk carving, or the carved cabriole leg and claw foot: the back is of open work of scrolls, strap-work, or ribbon-work, with delicate carving. Mathias Lock published a book on furniture in 1765 and 1768. In 1789 and 1794, A. Hepplewhite published a set of designs, which largely influenced contemporary furniture. Much of his work is refined and delicate in treatment and distinctive in form, such as his chairs with the shield-shaped backs. M. A. Pergolesi published a folio in 1777, and made some beautiful chairs for Robert Adam, with straight fluted legs and refined scrolled arms and back. Excellent chairs were made by Thomas Sheraton, with straight legs, turned, fluted, or enriched with delicate carving, or an inlay of coloured woods, and having a delightful reticence of form and treatment. Sheraton published in 1791 and 1793 a work on furniture.

CHIPPENDALE.   SHERATON.

Early Gothic tables were of the trestle form, the ends being of two pieces, connected by the upper frame and a lower stretcher. The Renascence table retained this form (figs. 1, 2, 4, and 5), which was but a survival of the Greek and Roman marble table (fig. 3). The Elizabethan table had legs of a bulbous form, gadrooned or carved, with upper and lower rails. The oval Gate-leg table, with spiral or turned legs, is characteristic of the early Stuart period. Chippendale frequently used the straight legs and carved or open rails, with a raised fret-work edge round the edge of the table. Sheraton's tables were frequently inlaid with different coloured woods, or of satin-wood veneer, painted with flowers or wreaths, and polished by hand. The ornament of Sheraton is seldom original, but founded upon that of Adams (plate 26), consisting of rosettes, urns, scrolls, and festoons. The artists Cipriani, and Angelica Kauffman, are known to have decorated furniture for the brothers Adam.

Early cupboards were of oak, with pierced and carved tracery panels, which were followed by the linen-fold panel, a favourite mode of enrichment from 1480 to 1560. In the early Renascence (plate 23), the Gothic and classic styles were intermingled, but a little later the panels were carved with medallion-heads and wreaths. This was followed by the classic furniture designed by the French architects Philibert de l'Orme, de Cerceau, who published a book on furniture in 1550 (fig. 2), and Jean Bullant, and the famous master *ébénistes* of the Renascence, of whom the best known is Andre Boule (1642-1702), who used a fine inlay of tortoise-shell and brass (" Boule work ") upon ebony or mahogany, enhanced with gilded bronze mounts.

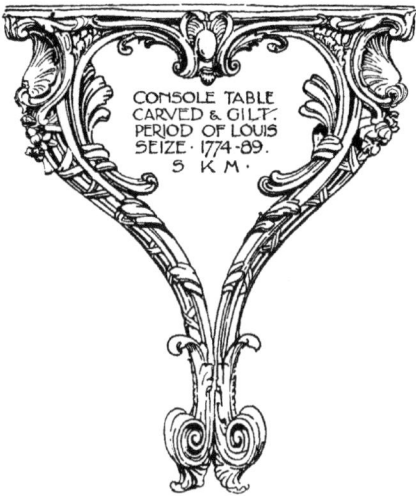

CONSOLE TABLE CARVED & GILT. PERIOD OF LOUIS SEIZE · 1774-89. S K M ·

In Louis XV.'s reign, Charles Cressent (1685-1768), a pupil of Boule, produced fine examples of " Boule work " and *appliqué* bronze enrichments. Other great *ébénistes* of this *Rocaille* period were Juste Aurèli Meissonier (1695-1750), and the brothers Slodtz, also Jacques Caffieri, a craftsman of extraordinary dexterity and caprice in metal mountings for furniture. Magnificent mahogany cabinets, enriched with marquetry, and Sèvres porcelain plaques were characteristic of this period, as was also some beautiful furniture by Robert Martin (1706-70) and his brothers, lacquered with a transparent green and gold lac (" Vernis Martin ").

With Louis XVI. and Marie Antoinette, a reaction set in for more restraint in ornament and severity of line and form, and the beautiful cabinets by Reisner and David Roentgen were remarkable for refined craftsmanship and beauty of ornamentation, with a marquetry of flowers, festoons, and diaper borders of rosewood, tulip, pear, and lime upon mahogany and ebony ; they were enhanced with bronze mountings by Gouthière, who was a renowned and skilful craftsman.

The Elizabethan and Jacobean periods were famous for their tester bedsteads, which have richly-carved panelled or arcaded backs, the tester also having elaborate panelling and carving. The baluster pillars at the foot usually have square bases, with pierced or open arcadings, and the slender pillars above have wide bulbous divisions, gadrooned or carved.

In Italy, during the 16th century, many beautiful *cassone*, or chests, were produced, enriched with carving (fig. 6), Gesso, and gilding, or painted by the great masters of the Renascence. Intarsia (an inlay of wood) was universal in Italy for the enrichment of the beautiful choir stalls of the 15th and 16th centuries.

CARVED FRAME IN
WALNUT, BY
ANTONIO BARILI.
Late 15TH Century
SIENA.

1

2

CENTRE OF CARVED TRIPTYCH BY VEIT STOSS.
SOUTH KENSINGTON MUSEUM.

3

A MISERERE. WESTMINSTER ABBEY.

4

CARVED MIRROR FRAME,
GRINLING GIBBONS. 1648-1721.
SOUTH KENSINGTON MUSEUM.

5

CARVED AND
GILT WOOD
PEDESTAL FOR A
CANDELABRUM
OR "GUERIDON".
PERIOD OF
LOUIS XIV.
S.K.M.

WOOD CARVING.

Wood carving is perhaps one of the earliest and most universal of the industrial arts. The splendid carved statues and statuettes found in the early tombs of Egypt, the vigorous reliefs of the spiral and dragon from the Scandinavian churches (plate 14), the intricate spirals of New Zealand (plate 1), the pierced and carved screens of India, the beautiful carving on the furniture of the Renascence (plate 45), and the delicate and skilful work of Grinling Gibbons bear tribute to the universal skill of craftsmanship, which reached its highest point of excellence in the later Gothic and Renascence period.

The choir stalls of Amiens Cathedral (plate 20) by Arnold Boulin, Alexander Huet, and Jean Turpin (1508-22), are magnificent examples of the versatility and skill of the flamboyant carver. But France was not alone in the excellence of this craft, for almost contemporaneous are the beautiful doors of the Stanza della Incendio and the Stanza della Eliodoro in the Vatican at Rome (see page 60), by Giovanni Barili, and the choir stalls in the Cathedral at Siena by Antonio and Giovanni Barili. The magnificent candelabra and the delicate carvings and intarsia in the choir of Sante Marie in Organo, at Verona, by Fra Giovanni da Verona, and the stalls and screen in Sante Maggiore, Bergamo, by Stephano da Bergamo, are some of the finest examples of wood carving in Italy. The richly carved oak stalls by Jörg Syrlin (1464-74) in the Cathedral at Ulm, indicate the beginning of the intricate and florid scroll-work, which became the type of the later German Renascence. The hanging screen and crucifix of S. Lawrence, and the crucifix at S. Sebald's at Nuremberg (1518), by Veit Stoss (fig. 2), are admirable examples of the skilful and florid carving of the German school during the early part of the 16th century.

In Flanders, the splendid chimney-piece in the Palais de Justice, Bruges, with carvings of Charles V. and his ancestors, by Guyot de Beaugrant, from designs by Blondell (1529-31), is rich, yet restrained in treatment, but in the pulpit of the Cathedral at Brussels, by Verbrüggen (1699), carved with figures and foliage, representing the expulsion from Paradise, and in the pulpit by Van de Voort in the Cathedral of Antwerp, carved with naturalistic birds, trees, and figures, extraordinary technical skill is attained, but with a loss of dignity and appropriateness of treatment.

Admirable examples, good in design and technique, abound in English cathedrals, in the screens, canopies, and misereres of the choir stalls (plates 19, 25, 45) of the 14th and 15th centuries.

With Grinling Gibbons (1648-1721) wood carving reached its culmination in delicacy and skilful craftsmanship (fig. 4), his principal works, consisting of flowers, festoons, and birds, are carved chiefly in lime, of which fine examples are at Belton House and Petworth ; and in collaboration with Sir Christopher Wren he executed splendid carvings in the library at Trinity College, Cambridge, S. Paul's Cathedral, S. James's, Piccadilly, the vestry of S. Lawrence, Jewry, and at Hampton Court Palace.

FIG 1

TRIPTYCH. FRENCH. 14TH CENTURY
SOUTH KENSINGTON MUSEUM.

2

ASSYRIAN PANEL WITH INCISED
ORNAMENT. BRITISH MUSEUM.

3

TANKARD & COVER. IVORY BODY
IN HIGH RELIEF. ITALIAN 16TH Century

4

HEAD OF A PASTORAL
STAFF FRENCH 14TH Cent.
SOUTH KENSINGTON
MUSEUM

5

TOP OF MIRROR CASE THE ELOPEMENT OF QUEEN
GUINEVER & SIR LAUNCELOT. FRENCH 14TH CENTURY
SOUTH KENSINGTON MUSEUM.

6

CENTRE OF BOOK COVER
BYZANTINE 6TH CENTURY
IN MILAN CATHEDRAL

7   SVMMACHORVM   8

ONE LEAF OF A ROMAN DIPTYCH. 3RD CENTURY
SOUTH KENSINGTON MUSEUM
THE COMPANION LEAF IN THE CLUNY MUSEUM

9

BYZANTINE DIPTYCH 4TH Cent.
BRITISH MUSEUM.
THE LARGEST KNOWN
IVORY PLAQUE.

LEAF OF
A CONSULAR
DIPTYCH.
OF THE CONSUL ANASTASIUS.
BYZANTINE 6TH CENTURY.
SOUTH KENSINGTON MUSEUM.

10

HANDLE OF KNIFE

FORK FROM
NURNBERG
MUSEUM
17 CENTURY.

136

VORIES,

Doubtless owing to their beautiful texture, colour and adaptability for delicate carving, have been in use from a remote period. Egypt, Assyria, and India have each contributed many beautiful examples of fine craftmanship, indicative of the artistic culture of the centuries preceding the Christian Era.

In the Periclean age of Greece, ivory was used for the figure of Athene Parthenos by Pheidias, placed inside the Parthenon. This statue of the standing goddess, 40 ft. high, was of gold and ivory (called *chryselephantine sculpture*), the drapery being of beaten gold and the exposed parts of the figure of carefully-fitted pieces of ivory. A seated *chryselephantine* figure of Jupiter, about 58 ft. high, in the temple of Olympia, was also by Pheidias. Pausanias, the Roman traveller, enumerates some ten *chryselephantine* statues which he saw in his travels (A.D. 140).

The Roman period is noted for the many beautiful Consular diptychs, which may now be seen in our national museums. They consist of two ivory leaves usually 12 by 5 in., the inside having a slightly sunk plane covered with wax for writing upon, the outside being enriched with delicate carved reliefs (figs. 7, 8, and 9). These diptychs were given by new consuls on their appointment, to their friends and officers of the state. The consul is usually represented seated on the cushioned curule chair, or chair of state, and his name is generally written across the top of one leaf.

The Byzantines enriched the covers of their manuscripts with ivory, of which an illustration is given in fig. 6; the ivory throne of Maximian, Archbishop of Ravenna (A.D. 546-556), is also of this period. A beautiful treatment of ivory was used in the 13th and 14th centuries by the Saracens of Egypt; they frequently worked a fine geometric inlay of ivory upon ebony; in other examples ivory panels were pentagonal, hexagonal, or star-shaped, and carved with delicate arabesques, the framing of the panels being of cedar or ebony. In India ivory carving reached a high degree of perfection, especially in the many ivory combs, with pierced and relief work representing the figure of Buddha surrounded with foliage and richly caparisoned elephants.

In the Carlovingian period, 8th to 10th centuries, ivory was largely used for coffers or small chests. During the early Gothic period in Italy and France, ivory crucifixes, pastoral staffs, croziers, statuettes, and triptychs were made in large numbers; and the ivory combs and mirror cases of the Renascence period have fine reliefs of legendary or allegorical subjects. Of pictorial ivories the modern Japanese craftsmen show the highest technical skill, combined with a keen perception of nature and movement, yet their ivories lack the beauty and dignity of composition and the decorative treatment of the early and Mediæval ivories.

1. IVORY BOOKCOVER. IX CENTURY
NORTH ITALY

2. PORTION OF A DURHAM
BINDING IN BROWN LEATHER.
BENEDICTINE MONASTERY. DURHAM.

3. STAMPED PANEL BY JEHAN NORINS.
1528.

4. STAMPED LEATHER BINDING. S^T GEORGE.
BY JOHN REYNES. 1520. ENGLISH

5. RED MOROCCO
BINDING
WITH GOLD
TOOLING.
Q CVRTIVS
THO MAIOLI
ET AMICOR
BOUND FOR TOMMASO MAIOLI

6. BINDING IN
YELLOW MOROCCO
TOOLED IN GOLD
CORYCIANA
IO·GROLIERII
ET AMICO
RVM
GROLIER BINDING.

7. RED MOROCCO
BINDING. TOOLED
IN GOLD BY
NICHOLAS EVE.

8. RED MOROCCO BINDING.
TOOLED WITH THE ARMS
& CYPHER OF LOUIS XIII

9. PORTION OF BLUE MOROCCO.
BINDING BOUND AND TOOLED
IN GOLD by ROGER PAYNE, 1795

OOKBINDINGS.

The covers used to protect manuscripts and printed books have always offered a suitable field for decoration, hence ornamental covers of various periods and materials are numerous. Ivory carved in relief or cut in open work, was frequently used for early Byzantine MS. (fig. 1). The chief material in use since the 10th century is leather, stamped with dies or tools. An early example dating from the 10th century is of red leather, with a raised interlacing Celtic design, and is now at Stonyhurst. Four remarkable leather bindings were executed at Durham for Bishop Pudsey (1153-95), stamped with small dies, of which there are over 50 varieties. Contemporaneous with these were similar stamped covers of the Winchester Domesday Book, produced at Winchester, and the Libre Sapientiae, at London. This tradition was continued in the 15th century at Oxford, and by Caxton (1477-91), who frequently used intersecting diagonal lines, between which small dies were placed. In the Low Countries and in Germany many beautiful bindings were produced by the panel stamp. The earliest English example has the Arms of Edward IV. impressed. Other fine examples are by F. Egmondt (1493), Richard Pynson (1520), and Jean Norris (1528), who used the acorn panel (fig. 3), and the S. George by John Reynes (fig. 4), who was binder with Thomas Berthelet (1542) to Henry VIII. The introduction of the *roll* in 1530 superseded the panel, and with the exception of those by Nicholas Spering, of Cambridge, these designs with Renascence figures and arcades are not to be compared for vitality and beauty of detail with those of the earlier period.

The gold tooling, which superseded the "blind tooling," was introduced from Saracenic sources into Europe at Venice, where, in 1488, Aldus Manutius commenced his fine series of printed books, and his early bindings (1500-10) had parallel lines and slight Arabian enrichments at the corners. Then followed the beautiful interlacing patterns that were executed for the famous book collectors, Tommaso Maioli (1507-59) and Count Grolier (1510-65, figs. 5, 6). The Royal bindings for Francis I. and Henry II. were by Peter Roffet, Philip le Noir, and Geoffrey Tory, who probably was also responsible for the Grolier bindings. The 17th century famous French binders were Nicholas and Clovis Eve (1578-1631, fig. 7), Macé Ruette, and Le Gascon, famous for his *pointillé* work. The 18th century binders were Boyet, N. and A. Padeloup and the Deromes, while the bindings of red morocco with broad tooled borders, executed for the Earl of Oxford (1710-41), known as the Harleian style, and the beautiful and refined bindings by Roger Payne (1795, fig. 9) are of contemporary English work.

The early Grolier tools were distinctly Arabian and solid or barred, while the bindings of "Eve" have interlacing circular and square panels with sprays of foliage. Some French bindings for Henry IV. are tooled with a *semis* of monograms or flowers.

EGYPTIAN FABRICS.
FROM AKHMÎM. 5TH OR 6TH CENTURY.
MANCHESTER COLLECTION.

EGYPTIAN FABRIC FROM AKHMÎM
6TH CENTURY.
SOUTH KENSINGTON MUSEUM.

SICILIAN 13TH CENTURY. S.K.M. SOUTH ITALIAN. 14TH CENTURY. S.K.M.

SICILIAN. 13TH CENTURY. S.K.M.

SILK DAMASK. SICILIAN. 13TH CENTURY.
SOUTH KENSINGTON MUSEUM.

SICILIAN. 13TH CENTURY.
MANCHESTER COLLECTION.

SICILIAN. 13TH CENTURY.
BOCK COLLECTION. MANCHESTER.

VENETIAN. FROM A PERSIAN DESIGN.
15TH CENTURY.

TEXTILE FABRICS.

The utility, universality, construction, texture, ornamentation, and colour of textile fabrics are full of interest and suggestiveness, for in the remarkable development of textile fabrics we may trace the continuity of style and tradition, the intermingling of races and customs, and the grafting of religious ideas with the wealth and luxuriance of the past. All fabrics wrought in the loom are called textiles. They are broadly divided into three classes:— (1) Plain fabrics in which the warp and weft alternate equally; (2) those fabrics in which a pattern is produced by the warp and weft intermingling in different proportions or colours, figured cloths and tapestries being included in this class; (3) those fabrics in which the plain textile No. 1 is enriched with the needle or by printing, termed embroideries or printed fabrics.

Owing to their perishable nature few remains of ancient textile fabrics are in existence. The oldest examples are found in the tombs of Egypt, where, owing to the dryness of the climate, some fabrics of the early dynasties still remain. They are usually of fine linen, and without enrichment, yet upon the same tombs are many painted patterns that undoubtedly show a woven origin. The oldest figured fabrics found in Egypt are of the 6th century A.D., and they show a remarkable similarity to the early patterns of Persia and Byzantium, for it was in India, Persia, and Arabia that textiles reached their perfection of workmanship, and their wealth of material. This splendid tradition was carried from Persia and India to Byzantium in the 5th century, and in the 8th century the Arabians absorbed and assimilated the arts of Persia, India, Egypt, and Spain, and brought the art of weaving to its culmination during the 14th and 15th centuries.

The ornamental designs of textile fabrics of different nations and periods are characterised by well-defined forms, differentiated by racial influence, climatic conditions and the myths and traditions of the people. Yet the traditional Eastern origin may be traced through many textile designs, for there is no doubt that India, Persia, and Arabia influenced the designs of textile fabrics more than other nations. This was due no doubt partly to the Eastern weavers carrying their art and traditions with them to various parts of Europe, and also to the exportation of their splendid fabrics, but principally to the beautiful and interesting designs, which were perfectly adapted to the process of weaving. It is due no doubt to this frank adaptation of natural forms and their appropriateness to the technical necessities of woven fabrics, that has rendered this Eastern influence so persistent through many centuries in different parts of Europe. It is remarkable that even in Italy during the whole of the Renascence period, with the characteristic scroll forms and acanthus foliation of its architecture and decorative arts, the textiles are quite distinct in style, having the characteristics of the Sicilian, Persian, and Indian ornament.

In the 12th century, Roger II., the Norman King of Northern Sicily, took Corinth and Argos, and carried many weavers and embroiderers from Greece to Sicily, and established them at Palermo, where they quickly assimilated the Sicilian style, and produced many fine fabrics during the 13th and 14th centuries.

The crusades now began to influence the arts. In 1098, Antioch was taken, and the spoil distributed through Europe. In 1204, Constantinople was taken by Baldwin, Count of Flanders, and the Venetian Doge, Dandolo, and the vast spoil of textiles distributed. It was doubtless under the influence of the crusades that the Sicilian weavers of the 13th and 14th centuries produced the many beautiful fabrics enriched with winged lions, foliated crosses and crowns, rayed stars, harts and birds linked together, and with the introduction of armorial bearings. Early in the 14th century this splendid tradition was introduced into Italy, and at Lucca many beautiful fabrics were produced, having the same characteristics and technique as the Sicilian fabrics.

SICILIAN FABRIC.

The cloak upon the recumbent bronze figure of Richard II., in Westminster Abbey, has a pattern of foliage, with couchant harts and rayed stars, and was most probably copied from the original silk made for Richard at Lucca or Palermo.

The beautiful materials and designs of Indian textile fabrics are indicative of the love of nature and the splendour of colour of a remote antiquity. Though influenced at various times by Greek, Persian, and Arabian traditions, India still preserved an indigenous ornamental art of remarkable freshness and vitality, the designers choosing their own flora and fauna with rare selective power and adaptive qualities. With an instinctive feeling for ornamental art, aided by the splendid colourings of the native dyes, they produced textile fabrics of silks, brocades, and gold and silver lace remarkable for richness and perfection of material, beauty of design, and harmony of colour.

The Indian pine is a familiar form of enrichment, differentiated

Plate 50.

PRINTED COTTON·
INDIAN 18ᵀᴴCᴇɴᵀʸ
S·K·M·

from the cypress of Persia (fig. 1, plate 29) by the spiral at the apex. This typical pine is treated with a wonderful diversity of detail (figs. 4, 5, and 6, plate 30). The splendid carpets of India were doubtless influenced by the Persian tradition, and they follow the same methods and ornamental arrangements, adapting, conventionalizing, and emphasising plants, flowers, and seeds, and rendering them with a fine feeling for form and colour. Block printing was largely used for silks and cottons, and many splendid examples are now treasured in our museums. An illustration of a printed cotton Palampore from South Kensington is given on the previous page, showing the beautiful floral treatment, diversity of detail, and contrast of line and mass. The gold and silver brocades, or " Kincobs," of Ahmedabad and Benares, with patterns of animals, flowers, and foliage richly spangled, the delicate muslins of Dacca, the gold and silver printed muslins of Jaipur, and the woollen shawls of Kashmir with the well-known pine pattern, are splendid examples of richness of material, delicacy and skilfulness of technique, and beauty and appropriateness of ornamentation.

The pile carpets of Persia, especially those of Kurdistan, Khorassan, Kirman, and Ferahan, are the finest in the world, being magnificent in colour and having bold conventional patterns of their beautiful flora, with birds and animals interspersed with the ornament, giving a largeness of mass and interest and vitality of detail. The hyacinth, tulip, iris, and the pink are frequently introduced, together with the hom, or tree of life. An illustration is given (fig. 2, plate 29) of a Genoa fabric, but of Persian design, showing the typical " pink " with its simplicity and beauty of line. This traditional art of Persia had a most marked influence upon the textile fabrics of Europe from the 12th to the 17th centuries. This was no doubt due to many causes; but the perfect adaptability to the process of weaving, the interest, inventiveness, and beauty of the ornament, and the singular frank treatment of form and colour, doubtless appealed to the craftsmen of Europe, and hence we find many Persian designs produced in Sicily, Spain, Italy, France, and Flanders.

The finest silk velvets and damasks produced from the looms of Florence show a distinct Persian influence in their bold artichoke and pomegranate patterns of the 16th and 17th centuries. In Genoa, similar patterns in many coloured velvets were produced, and it is singular how largely this persistency of type prevails in all countries.

In 1480, Louis XI. introduced the art into France, when looms were established at Tours, and in 1520 they were established at Lyons by Francis I., and the art of weaving rapidly spread. The earliest fabrics of these looms have patterns similar to the Persian and Italian fabrics; but soon the vase pattern, which no doubt had its origin in Byzantine textiles and which had been used by the Persians and Italians, began to influence French designs.

However, this rapidly gave place, towards the middle of the 17th century, to the imitation of ribbons and laces in textile fabrics, together with a more naturalistic treatment of floral forms, and the beauty, suggestiveness, and interest of the early patterns now gave way to prettiness, affectation, and a naturalistic treatment which culminated in the period of Madame Pompadour.

The remarkable invention of perforated cards for facilitating the weaving of figured fabrics was introduced by Bonchon (1725), and continued by Falcon in 1728, by Vancanson in 1745, and perfected by Joseph Marie Jacquard (1752-1834).

DESIGN FOR A
SPITALSFIELD
SILK FABRIC
DATED 1739.
S K M

The revocation of the Edict of Nantes in 1685 by Louis XIV. caused numbers of weavers to come to England, bringing their art and tradition with them, and many established themselves at Spitalfields, which soon rose to some importance. The patterns, necessarily, were purely French in treatment, consisting of natural arrangements of flowers.

The textile fabrics of Flanders reached a high degree of perfection in the 16th and 17th centuries, Bruges being famous for its silk damasks and velvets, the patterns showing the traditional Persian, or the pomegranate and artichoke type of the Florentine textiles.

Block printing had been introduced into Flanders in the 15th century, and many fine patterns with Indian motives were produced up to the 17th century.

At Ypres, fine diapered linen was manufactured, and Ghent was famous for its woollens, but the remarkable prosperity of Flanders was destroyed by the Spanish occupation (1556-1648).

Then large numbers of Flemish weavers came to England and settled in many parts of the country, bringing their traditions and craftsmanship, which have undoubtedly had a most marked influence upon the production of cotton and woollen textile fabrics in England.

Tapestry, of which many fine examples of the 16th and 17th centuries are treasured in our museums and palaces, differs from most woven fabrics in its method of production, which consists of interweaving and knotting short pieces of coloured wefts, which form the pattern, to a strong warp, a ground weft being thrown across each pick to bind the material well together.

This is almost the same method as that used in the manufacture of the Indian and Persian carpets. It was during the 14th and 15th centuries, at Arras in Flanders, that storied tapestries were brought to their culmination, and the tapestry workers became a most powerful

Plate 51.

WHITE SILK
DAMASK.
LYONS.
XVII Century

GREEN SILK
DAMASK
LYONS
XVII Century

146

guild. From about 1480, Brussels produced many magnificent hangings from designs by the great masters of the Italian Renascence. Raphael's famous cartoons, which are now in the South Kensington Museum, are the original designs for the ten tapestries manufactured at Brussels for Pope Leo X., for the enrichment of the Sistine Chapel in the Vatican ; the seven cartoons, three being lost, were purchased by Charles I.

Many of the great Flemish painters also designed for the Brussels tapestries, such as Van Orley, Van Leyden, and Jan Mabuse.

Francis I. caused tapestry looms to be set up at Fontainebleau in 1339, under the direction of the Italian, Serlio, but it was not until the Gobelin tapestry manufactory was established in 1603 in the Faubourg Saint Marcel by the Fleming, Marc de Comans, and François de la Planche, that French tapestry reached any importance. Under the Minister Colbert in 1667, the Royal Gobelin manufactory produced many fine tapestries designed by the head of the establishment, Charles le Brun.

About 1590, some carpets, called Savonnerie, were made in the Louvre, the technique being somewhat similar to the Persian carpets, but the patterns were more pictorial and naturalistic in treatment. Fine tapestries were also produced at Beauvais and Aubusson. Tapestry had been manufactured in England as early as the reign of Edward III., but it was not until the time of James I. that it assumed any importance, when a tapestry manufactory was established at Mortlake by Francis Crane.

Some fine Flemish tapestries are in the South Kensington Museum, and eight large pieces by Bernard Van Orley are in the Great Hall of Hampton Court. The coloured cartoons by Mantegna in Hampton Court, representing the Triumph of Cæsar, were to be reproduced in tapestry for the Duke of Mantua. There are some fine Gobelin and Beauvais tapestries in Windsor Castle which were gifts from the Court of France, and they all show the most consummate technique, beauty of material, and harmony of colour. The well-known Bayeux tapestry is embroidered in coloured wools upon a white linen ground. It is 214 ft. in length and 22 inches in width, and divided in 72 compartments, with incidents representing the Norman invasion of England by William I. Though reputed to be the work of Queen Matilda, the probability is that it is the work of English hands some few years after the invasion. This embroidery or tapestry is still preserved in the Cathedral of Bayeux.

The remarkable civilization of the Incas or Peruvians is shown in the many splendid objects of the industrial arts now treasured in our museums. Of these relics of a vanished civilization, the textile fabrics are perhaps the most instructive and interesting. The high technical skill of the craftsmanship, the fine spinning of the wool and cotton, and the perfection of the dyeing of the yarn, together with the skilful weaving of the figured cloths and tapestries, are a tribute

BROCATELLE ITALIAN 16TH CENTURY.
S.K.M

SINGLE MULLION PATTERN.
FLEMISH 16TH CENTURY

FLOWER-VASE PATTERN. LATE
16TH CENTURY VENETIAN.
BOCK COLLECTION MANCHESTER

DOUBLE MULLION PATTERN. ITALIAN
16TH CENTURY. MANCHESTER BOCK COLLECTION

VELVET FROM GENOA FROM A PERSIAN
DESIGN. 16TH CENTURY. S.K.M.

VELVET. ITALIAN 16TH CENTURY
MUSÉE DES ARTS DECORATIFS. PARIS.

SILK ITALIAN. 16TH CENTURY.

SILK BROCADE. 18TH CENTURY.

FIGD SATIN. 18TH CENTURY. LYONS.

to the vitality and civilization of a people remote from all Asiatic or European influences.

These Peruvian textiles are remarkable for the absence of the beautiful flora of Peru as elements for decoration. The fret is a frequent form of enrichment. The wave scroll so typical of Greek work is also a remarkable element in Peruvian ornament, and illustrates the singular development of the same ideas and aspect of form among people so remote from each other as the Greeks and Peruvians. But the patterns that sharply differentiate Peruvian examples from all other styles are the conventional treatments of figures, birds, fishes, and animals. The llama is conspicuous in many patterns, but the bird forms are the most remarkable, having many variations of type and treatment.

TAPESTRY IN WHITE & BROWN.

DOUBLE CLOTH IN BROWN & YELLOW.

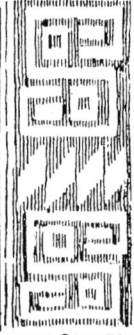

KEY PATTERN IN BROWN & YELLOW

DOUBLE CLOTH IN BROWN & YELLOW.

It is difficult to fix any date for these Peruvian examples, but as it is known that during the reign of Inca Pachacutic (circa 1390) the ceramic art was at its best, we may assume that the sister art of weaving reached its perfection about the same period, and continued until the Spanish Conquest in the 16th century.

Many of the fabrics are of double cloth, of deep brown and pale straw colour, and show the same colour and pattern on both sides of the cloth. Some of the fabrics are tapestry woven, having short strands of coloured wool inserted into the fabric by the aid of the needle, and they somewhat resemble the Gobelin tapestry in their method of production.

149

TERMS USED IN ORNA-MENTAL ART.

Ornament is the means by which Beauty or Sig nificance is imparted to Utility. It is either Symbolical or Æsthetic. Symbolic ornament consists of elements or forms chosen for the sake of their *significance*—Æsthetic ornament consists of forms or elements chosen for their *Beauty* alone, or their power of appealing to the senses.

Of the historic styles of ornament, the Egyptian, Assyrian, Byzantine, Scandinavian, Persian, Indian, Gothic, Polynesian, and much of the Chinese and Japanese are symbolical, having elements and ornamental details chosen for their significance; while in the Greek, Roman, and Renascence ornament the purely æsthetic motive is characteristic.

Ornament, again, may be natural or conventional—Imitative or Inventive. The terms "natural" and "imitative" have the same significance—*viz.*, the exact copying of natural forms, so that they become principal, not secondary as perfect ornament should be. Conventional ornament is the adaptation of natural forms to ornamental and technical requirements, and is seen in its greatest beauty in the frank treatment by the Indians and Persians of their flora and fauna for the decorative enrichment of their textile fabrics, pottery, and jewellery.

Inventive ornament is that which consists of elements not derived from any natural source; the Moresque style is a good example of this type.

The *elements* of ornament are the details or forms chosen for ornamental motives, and the *principals* of ornament are the arrangement of these forms and details; they comprise repetition, alternation, symmetry, radiation, balance, proportion, variety, eurythmy, contrast, intersection, complication, fitness, and utility.

Repetition is the use of elements in a continuous series; *Alternation* is the repetition of an element at intervals, with others intervening; *Symmetry*: when the leading lines are equal or similar (or reciprocal) on both sides; *Radiation*: when the lines spring from a centre, for example, a bird's wing and the flower of the daisy; *Balance* and *Proportion*: when the relation and harmony of parts is based upon natural laws; *Variety* implies difference in the details, with respect to form or type; *Eurythmy* signifies rhythms or harmony in ornament; *Contrast* is the arrangement in close proximity of colours or forms of opposite characters, as the straight line with the curve, or light with dark; *Intersection* is the crossing of the leading lines, the Arabian, Moresque and Celtic styles are examples of this principle; *Complication* is the effect produced by elements so arranged as to be more or less difficult to trace with the eye alone: as in the Japanese key and the Moresque star pattern. *Fitness* and *utility* as their names imply are essentials in all good periods of ornamentation.

PRINTED INITIAL LETTERS.

The initial letter, with its beauty of line and colour, its emphasis and distinctive character, was a frequent form of enrichment to the beautiful early manuscripts, and when, in the latter part of the 15th century, the printed book began to supersede the MS., the "Illuminator," or rubricator, was still called upon to enrich the printed page with his beautiful initials. Frequently, however, the rubricator was not called upon, with the result that many of the early printed books are still without their intended initial letters, as we find in many of the magnificent folios issued from the Aldine Press at Venice about 1500.

When the printed initial first made its appearance, it necessarily followed the type and character of the illuminated examples, as in the fine B (page 31), from the Mainz Psalter[1] in red and black, and which is the earliest example known (1457), printed with the text, and this initial is distinctly based upon the earlier illuminated capital.

Illustrations are given on pages 5, 7, 9, 21, 81, 93, 107, 131 of eight beautiful printed initials from the "Suetonius" of 1740[1] by the Germans, Conrad Sweynheym and Arnold Pannartz, who in 1456 introduced the art of printing into Italy, at the Benedictine Monastery at Subiaco, near Rome. These initials, with their distinctive and refined Roman type, and delicate interlacing scrolls, are admirable examples of the early printed initial. They were afterwards acquired by Riessinger, who used them in 1480-98 for his printed books at Rome. The five examples, with well-designed interlacings, given on pages 35, 37, 53, 85, 91 are taken from the fine "Euclid" by Ratdolt, of Venice, printed in 1481.[1] Three excellent initials from the beautiful printed books by Aldus Manutius, at Venice,[1] are given on pages 3, 87, 113.

Well-designed Gothic initials are given on page 13 from the "Fasciculus Temporum" (1481) by Ratdolt of Venice, the D (page 49) by Antonios Campigollis (1475), and the N from the "Life of Campanus," by M. Feronis, at Milan (1495, page 38). Eight beautiful Gothic initials given on pages 25, 73, 125, 135, 141, 153, 154, and preface, having well-spaced convential foliage and flowers, are taken from "Froissarts Cronycles," printed in London by Richard Pynson (1523).[1] Other examples are the two from the Golden Bible (pages 33, 95) and the C on page 97 from the "Missale Traijectense" (1515), showing an intricate interlacing of the letter itself, the same characteristic appearing in the Romaunt of the Rose given on pages 69, 111, 117, 139, and in the preface.

Two rich examples of foliated initials by Israel van Meckenen (1500), are given on pages 55 and 79. The P on page 29 is from Venice (1498); the N, page 45, is dated 1510; the G, page 121, is from the Flemish woodcut alphabet of 1464 (British Museum); and the T on page 150 is from the Basle woodcut copy of this alphabet.

The Italian examples on pages 127 and 151 illustrate the decorative use of the figure in the early 16th century initials.

[1] From the original editions in the John Rylands Library.

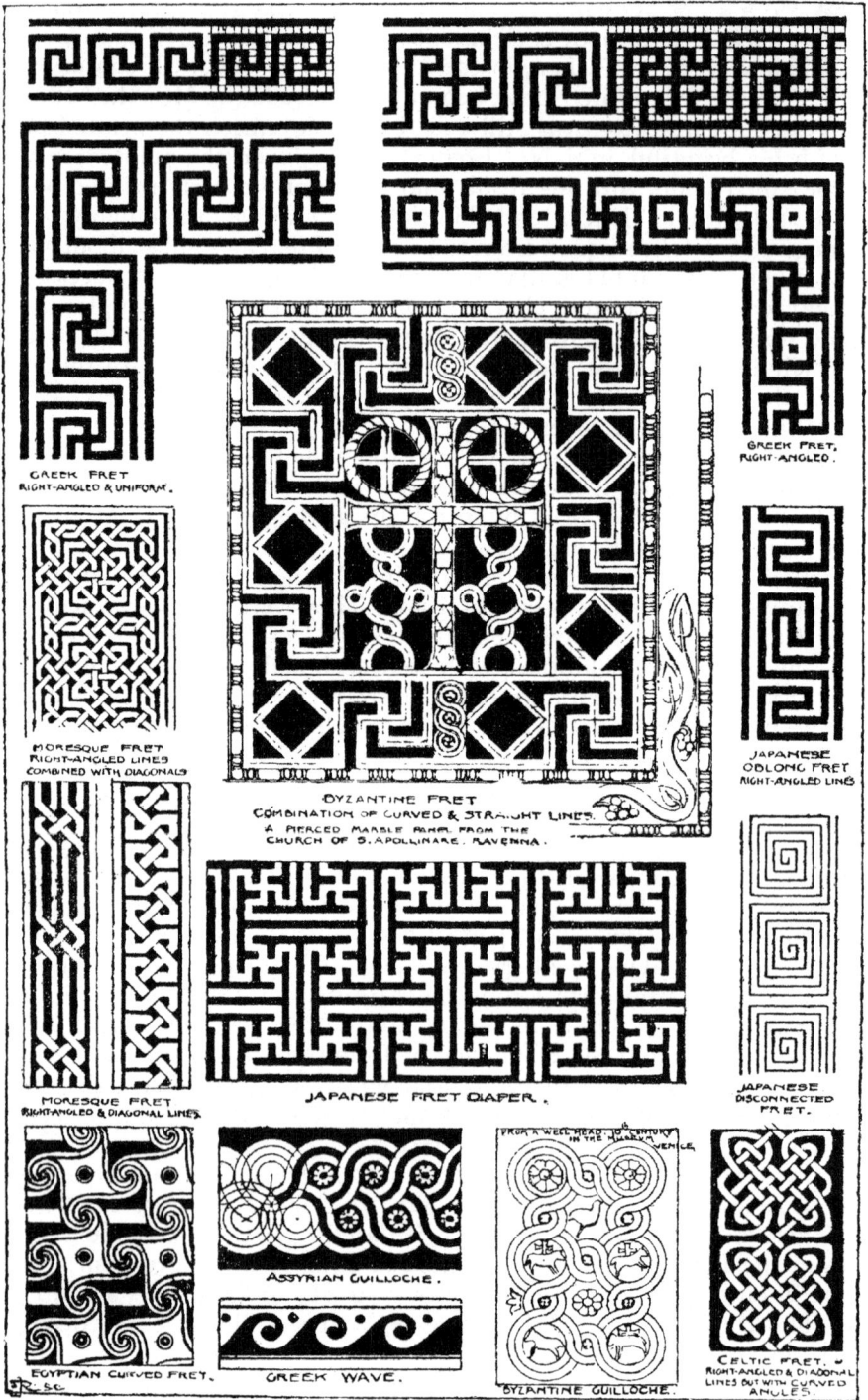

GREEK FRET
RIGHT-ANGLED & UNIFORM.

MORESQUE FRET
RIGHT-ANGLED LINES
COMBINED WITH DIAGONALS

MORESQUE FRET
RIGHT-ANGLED & DIAGONAL LINES

EGYPTIAN CURVED FRET.
R.sc

BYZANTINE FRET
COMBINATION OF CURVED & STRAIGHT LINES.
A PIERCED MARBLE PANEL FROM THE
CHURCH OF S. APOLLINARE. RAVENNA.

JAPANESE FRET DIAPER.

ASSYRIAN GUILLOCHE.

GREEK WAVE.

FROM A WELL HEAD. 10TH CENTURY
IN THE MUSEUM VENICE

BYZANTINE GUILLOCHE.

GREEK FRET,
RIGHT-ANGLED.

JAPANESE
OBLONG FRET
RIGHT-ANGLED LINES

JAPANESE
DISCONNECTED
FRET.

CELTIC FRET.
RIGHT-ANGLED & DIAGONAL
LINES BUT WITH CURVED
ANGLES.

FRETS.

The remarkable universality of the fret, the simplicity and rhythm of detail, its adaptability and usefulness for surface enrichment, have made the fret one of the best known forms of ornamentation. It was used in the surface decorations of the tombs of Egypt, the temples of Greece, and the civic and domestic buildings of Rome.

The Greek form with its right-angular and equally-spaced keys, was used on the simple abacas and plain fascias of the Dorian architecture, in bands upon the painted vases, and in a concentric form when used in the interior of the red-figured circular cylix. The Romans, without imparting freshness used the same right-angled key-pattern, chiefly as borders for mosaic pavements and upon the horizontal soffits of their architecture. The Byzantine, using the same type in conjunction with the cross and circle, gave more significance to the fret.

The Arabian fret differs in the use of the oblique line, together with the right angled key, obtaining a wonderful degree of complexity and richness.

The Celtic fret is chiefly a diagonal one but the recurrent angle is rounded to a curve.

Chinese and Japanese frets are usually right-angled, and are used in great profusion, often in a secondary field or background.

The Japanese key or "*Fret diaper*" is used in the greatest profusion; it is used alike on silks and brocades, damascened

WALL-MOSAIC OF COLOURED MARBLES

in metal, in cloisonné enamel and in lacquered work, and is frequently arranged in irregular shaped compartments or medallions.

The Greek continuous fret border is rarely used by the Japanese who generally use the disconnected or irregular fret. A similar irregular fret border was used by the Peruvians (page 101 and 147), by the Mexicans, and by the natives of Polynesia.

The Assyrian and Byzantine guilloche is but a curved fret, but additional interest is given by the introduction of radiating forms in the principal interstices of the fret.

The simplest form of construction for frets, or key pattern, is to use squared or ruled paper. The Chinese or Japanese key is comparatively simple to construct by making the double T 17 squares in length with arms at each end of 13 squares, and placed alternately at right angles to each other.

THE ARCHITECTURAL CAPITAL.

The form and enrichment of the Architectural Capital offer one of the most interesting and instructive fields of study in the history and evolution of architecture and ornament. The remarkable persistency of the capital as a distinctive feature in architecture may be traced through many centuries, though differentiated by climatic conditions and racial influences, yet still preserving a remarkable similarity of form and enrichment among the various nations of the earth.

The function of the capital is to sustain and transmit to the columns the weight of the entablature or archivolt, and the beauty and appropriateness of the capital depends (1) upon this functional treatment of strength; (2) upon the beauty of profile or mass; (3) upon the enrichment and proportion of the capital.

The dignified Doric capital of the Greeks illustrates these functions and conditions by its perfect adaptability, simple functional strength, beauty of profile, appropriateness of enrichment and proportion and harmony of parts, qualities which are essential to beauty of architecture. In the Parthenon (B.C. 438) we have the finest treatment of this capital—a treatment full of dignity, reserve, and unison of profile (plate 4). The many examples of the Doric Order in Greece and her colonies attest to the esteem in which this order was held by the Greeks. The Indian capital (plate 30) exhibits the same functional treatment by the use of brackets or modillions, which undoubtedly are a survival of a wooden construction, and which are typical of Eastern architecture.

The remarkable persistency of the profile and enrichment of the capital extending through a period of 4,000 years may be illustrated by a series of diagrams of typical examples. The profile of the capital has not varied to any appreciable extent in the examples here given, and the enrichment of the bell is remarkable for its persistency, though differentiated by racial influences. The Corinthian capital, with its volutes and acanthus foliage, is but the architectural continuity of the Egyptian capital. The only pure Greek example of this order is from the monument of Lysicrates, but the Romans continued the tradition, assimilating and elaborating until they produced the magnificent capitals of the portico of the Pantheon and the temple of Castor and Pollux. In these examples the leaves are arranged in series of two rows of eight leaves each, the volutes springing from sheaths and stems between the leaves which support the angle of the volutes. The

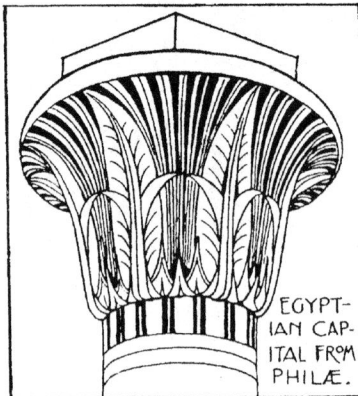

EGYPTIAN CAPITAL FROM PHILÆ.

example of early French Gothic has similar characteristics and illustrates the continuity of style.

The Ionic capital (page 10), though one of the most persistent in the history of architecture, never reached the architectonic perfection of other capitals. This was undoubtedly owing to the wooden origin being incompatible with the necessities of stone and marble. There is a want of unity between the volutes and ovolo of the capital; in brief, it has neither coherence nor harmony of parts. The exquisite craftsmanship of the capitals of the Erectheum, with their anthemion enrichment of the greatest purity, the beauty of the ovolo and the subtility of the volutes compensates to some extent for the lack of unison (plate 4). The enrichment of the architectural capital is no doubt a survival of the primitive custom of binding floral forms round the simple functional capital, these forms being afterwards perpetuated in stone or marble.

In early Corinthian examples these floral forms were frequently of beaten metal, which, in turn, gave place to the beautiful marble foliage of the Greeks and Romans.

That the ancients used metal work in their capitals we have abundant proof. In the descriptions of the building of Solomon's Temple we read of "Two chapiters of molten brass to set upon the pillars, and nets of chequer work and wreath of chain work to set upon the top of the pillars."

The composite capital is deficient in coherence and unity of parts, having the same defects as its prototype the Ionic. The annexed illustration from Ancient Rome gives an unusual treatment by the introduction of the human figure in the centre of the face of the capital.

The Byzantine capital differs from those of the Greeks and Romans in its marked symbolism of detail and the prevalence of the cushion form. Functionally, this type of capital is admirable, yet it lacks the vigorous upward growth of the Egyptian and early Gothic capitals.

155

The Byzantine capitals have a wonderful complexity and variety of detail, such as interlacing circles and crosses with their mystic symbolism, basket work, chequered details, and the traditional sharp acanthus foliage of the Greeks.

These features are seen in the greatest profusion at S. Sofia at Constantinople; S. Apollinare and S. Vitale at Ravenna, and S. Marco at Venice. These splendid capitals of a splendid period are exceedingly beautiful in fertile inventiveness of enrichment, and show the assimilative power of the Byzantine craftsmen. The abundant use of chequer work, wreaths of chain work, and of lily work in Byzantine capitals, many of which are figured in Ruskin's "Stones of Venice," show the continuity of style and tradition in architecture.

The Byzantine capitals have the square abacus, usually consisting of a simple fillet and chamfer enriched with the billet, dentil or star pattern. The Dosseret, a singular adjunct to the capital, was introduced during this period; it was a cushion-shaped or cubicle stone placed upon the abacus of the capital to give additional height (plate 11).

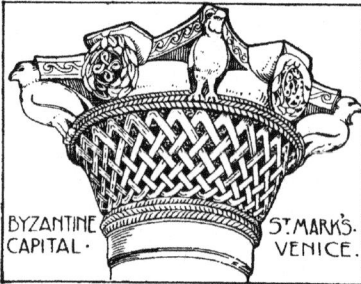

The Byzantine influence is seen upon the Norman capitals with their square abacus of fillet and chamfer, and the cushion profile of capital. Some remarkable Siculo-Norman capitals are in the cloisters of the Benedictine Monastery of Monreale in Sicily (A.D. 1174-1184). The great fertility of inventiveness in the 200 capitals, their storiation, the intermingling of figures, birds and animals with the classic and Byzantine foliage makes this cloister one of the most remarkable in the history of the world. The Arabian capital, which frequently shows the traditional volute, differs from the typical bell-shaped form in its marked squareness of profile with flat or low reliefs enriched with colour.

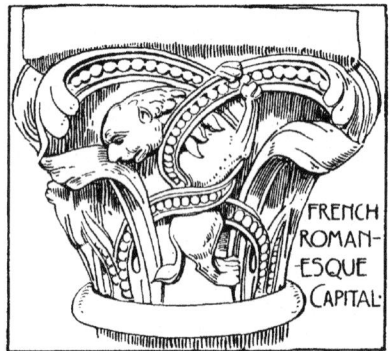

The early Gothic capital is one of the most vigorous and beautiful.

156

The perfect adaptability of its foliage to stone carving, the signifi-

CAPITALS FROM THE CLOISTERS MONREALE

cance of its detail as emble-
matic of the Trinity, the spiral
growth of its foliage, and the
vigorous contrast of light and
shade are the chief characteristics of this period. Lacking,
perhaps, the delicacy or variety
of detail of the Byzantine
period, or the later Gothic
work, it excelled them in the
appropriateness of its enrichment, which is more beautiful
in the early English examples with their circular abacus than in

CAPITALS FROM THE CLOISTERS OF MONREALE

contemporary French capitals
where the square abacus was
prevalent. The transition from
the circular column to the
square abacus was always felt
to be a difficulty, and was
rarely overcome, but in the
circular abacus of the early
English capitals we have a
break in the continuity of the
style of the capital.

The English foliage of this
period differs from the French in the use of a deep mid-rib and simple

EARLY ENGLISH CAPITAL

ELY CATHE-DRAL.

ARABIAN CAPITAL FROM THE ALHAMBRA

trefoil leaf. The French examples have a less pronounced mid-rib,
and the leaf is convex in form and divided into three lobes, and the
foliage adheres more closely to the bell, consequently the brilliant
play of light and shade which is so characteristic of early English
work, is generally absent from French examples (fig. 12, plate 17).

The decorated Gothic capitals differ essentially from those of the early Gothic period, a more natural type of foliage being used, consisting of the briony, maple, mallow, and oak. This foliage was

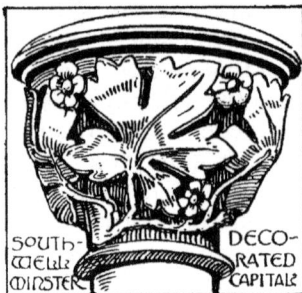

SOUTH-WELL MINSTER DECORATED CAPITAL

carved with singular delicacy of touch and grace of profile, and is beautiful in its modelling and play of light and shade, yet frequently the capitals are trivial in conception and arrangement, lacking that architectonic character which is so essential to all architectural constructive features.

The perpendicular, or late Gothic capital, was usually octagonal in form with square conventional foliage of the vine, showing a marked decadence in tradition and craftsmanship.

14ᵗʰ CENTURY CAPITAL. CHARTRES.

The Renascence capital was frequently marked by a fine feeling for profile, splendid craftsmanship, diversity of enrichment, and vitality of conception, more especially in Italy, where the tradition of architecture culminated in the works of such remarkable men as Leon Battista Alberti, Bramante, Baldassare Peruzzi, San Micheli, Serlio, Palladio, and Sansovino.

The tradition was worthily carried on in France by Pierre Lescot,

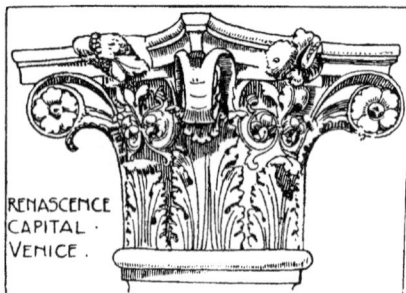

RENASCENCE CAPITAL. VENICE.

Jean Bullant, Philibert de Lorme, and De Brosse, and in England by Inigo Jones, Wren, and Chambers.

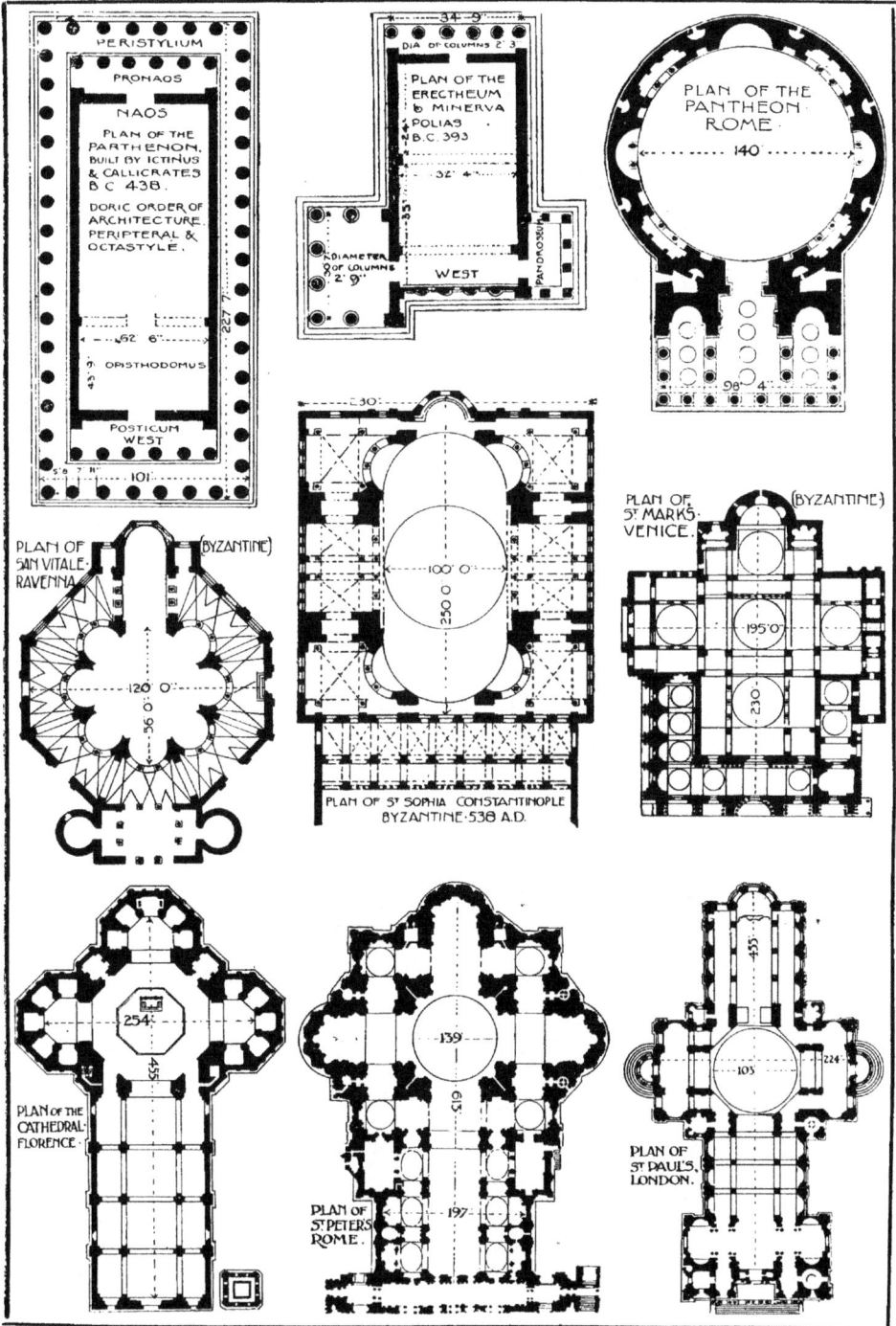

PERISTYLIUM

PRONAOS

NAOS

PLAN OF THE
PARTHENON.
BUILT BY ICTINUS
& CALLICRATES
B C 438.

DORIC ORDER OF
ARCHITECTURE.
PERIPTERAL &
OCTASTYLE.

OPISTHODOMUS

POSTICUM
WEST

101

PLAN OF THE
ERECTHEUM
& MINERVA
POLIAS.
B.C. 393

DIA OF COLUMNS 2' 3"

DIAMETER
OF COLUMNS
2' 9"

WEST

PLAN OF THE
PANTHEON.
ROME.
140

98' 4"

PLAN OF
SAN VITALE.
RAVENNA.

(BYZANTINE)

120' 0"

PLAN OF ST SOPHIA. CONSTANTINOPLE
BYZANTINE · 538 A.D.

100' 0"

250' 0"

PLAN OF
ST MARKS.
VENICE.

(BYZANTINE)

195' 0"

230

PLAN OF THE
CATHEDRAL.
FLORENCE.

254

455

PLAN OF
ST PETERS
ROME.

139

615

197

PLAN OF
ST PAUL'S,
LONDON.

455

103

224

PAGE FROM ONE OF THE HARLEIAN MANUSCRIPTS,
BRITISH MUSEUM,
FRENCH, EARLY 15TH CENTURY.

160

THE TWO "FATES," FROM THE
EASTERN PEDIMENT OF
THE PARTHENON.

CARYATIDE
FROM THE
ERECTHEUM.

CLASSIC SCULPTURE—GOTHIC SCULPTURE:
A COMPARISON.

CENTRAL PIER &
PART OF TYMPANUM
FROM THE SOUTH
DOOR OF AMIENS
CATHEDRAL
13TH CENTURY.

FIGURES FROM THE WEST
FRONT OF CHARTRES
CATHEDRAL. 12TH CENTURY

TEXT-BOOKS UPON ARCHITECTURE AND ORNAMENT.

			s.	d.
Architecture of the Renascence in Italy	*W. J. Anderson,*		12	6
Classic and Early Christian Architecture	*Roger Smith,*		5	o
Gothic and Renascence	*Roger Smith,*		5	o
Glossary of Architecture	*J. Parker,*		7	6
History of Architecture	*Fletcher,*		21	o
Introduction to Gothic Architecture	*J. Parker,*		5	o
Three Manuals of Gothic Ornament	*J. Parker,*	each	1	o
Classic and Early Christian Sculpture	*G. Redford,*		5	o
Gothic and Renascence Sculpture	*Leader Scott,*		5	o
English Architecture	*J. D. Atkinson,*		3	6
Handbook of Greek Sculpture, 2 vols.	*Ed. Gardner,*		10	o
History of Greek Art	*Tarbell,*		5	o
Analysis of Ornament	*J. Wornum,*		8	o
Handbook of Ornament	*Meyer,*		12	6
Pattern Design	*Lewis F. Day,*		7	6
Ornament and its Application	,,		8	6
The Bases of Design	*Walter Crane,*		6	o
Line and Form	,,		6	o
History of Art (Revised by *Russell Sturgis*)	*Lubke,*		36	o
Principles of Ornament	*G. W. Rhead,*		6	o
Bibliotheque de l'Ensignement des Beaux-Arts (various subjects)	*Paris,*	each vol.	4	o

An excellent series of illustrated hand-books upon the Industrial Arts, by writers of repute, is published by the Science and Art Department, and may be obtained at the bookstall of the South Kensington Museum, at a cost of 1s. each part (paper covers), or they may be purchased through Messrs. Chapman and Hall, at 2s. 6d. each part, bound in cloth. They include :—

Each in two parts.

The Industrial Arts of—
India.
Spain.
Denmark.
Scandinavia.
The Saracens of Egypt.
Early Christian Art in Ireland.
English Earthenware.
,, Porcelain.
French Pottery.
Wrought Iron Work.

Complete in one part.

Bronzes.
College and Corporation Plate.
Furniture.
Gold and Silversmith's Work.
Glass.
Stained Glass.
Ivories.
Japanese Pottery.
,, Colour Prints.
Maiolica.
Persian Art.
Textile Fabrics.
Tapestry.
The Industrial Arts.

The illustrated articles in the *Transactions* of the Royal Institute of British Architects may also be studied with advantage ; they include :—Byzantine Architecture, 1892 ; Casting in Metals, 1892 ; Decorative Plaster Work, 1891 ; Heraldry, 1897-8 ; Mosaics, 1894 ; Metal Work, 1906 ; Precious Windows of Chartres, 1906 ; Romanesque Architecture, 1901 ; Sculpture in relation to Architecture, 1891 ; Woodcarving, 1896-1906 ; Wrought Iron Work, 1891.

WORKS OF REFERENCE.

ARCHITECTURE.

A History of Architecture . . . . . *Fletcher.*
A History of Renascence Architecture in England . *Reginald Blomfield.*
Analysis of Gothic Architecture . . . . *R. & J. Brandon.*
Antiquities of Athens . . . . . . *Stuart and Revett.*
Antiquities of Rome . . . . . . *Taylor & Cresy.*
Architecture and Decoration of the Renascence
    in Italy . . . . *Schutz.*
Architecture : East and West . . . . *R. Phené Spiers.*
Architecture for General Readers . . . . *H. H. Statham.*
Architecture of Greece and Rome . *W. J. Anderson & R. Phené Spiers.*
Architecture of the Renascence in England . . *J. A. Gotch.*
Architecture of the Renascence in Italy . . . *W. J. Anderson.*
Architecture Toscane . . *A. Grandjean de Montigny & Famin.*
Byzantine Architecture . . . . . . *Texier & Pullan.*
    ,,   ,,   Constantinople . . . *Salzenberg.*
Dictionnaire Raisonné de l'Architecture Française . *Viollet le Duc.*
Early Renascence in England . . . . *J. A. Gotch.*
Examples of Greek and Pompeian Work . . *J. Cromar Watt.*
Fragments de l'Architecture Antique . . . *H. D'Espouy.*
    ,,   ,,   Renascence . . . ,,
French Renascence Detail . *The works of Daly, Sauvageot & Rouyer.*
Gothic Architecture . . . . . . *T. Rickman.*
Gothic Architecture in England . . . . *Francis Bond.*
Gothic Architecture in France . . . . *E. Corroyer.*
Gothic Details and Foliage . . . . . *J. K. Colling*
Gothic Mouldings . . . . . . *F. A. Paley.*
History of Architecture . . . . . *J. Ferguson.*
History of Gothic Art in England . . . . *E. S. Prior.*
Later English Renascence . . . . . *Belcher & Macartney.*
London Churches of the XVII. and XVIII. Centuries *G. H. Birch.*
Mansions of England . . . . . . *J. Nash.*
Old English Mansions . . . . . . *C. Richardson.*
Orders of Architecture . . *J. M. Mauch, C. Normand & R. P. Spiers.*
Palast Architektur, Toscana, Venedig . . *Raschdorff.*
    ,,   ,,   Genua . . . . . *R. Reinhardt.*
Parallels of English Abbey Churches . . . *E. Sharpe.*
Renascence Architecture in Spain . . . *A. N. Prentice.*
Rome, Renascence Buildings . . . . *Letarouilly.*
Rome, Baudenkmaeler des Alten . . . . *Strack.*
Seven Lamps of Architecture . . . . *J. Ruskin.*
Seven Periods of English Church Architecture . *E. Sharpe.*
Some Architectural Works of Inigo Jones . *H. I. Triggs & H. Tanner.*
Stones of Venice . . . . *J. Ruskin.*
Venezia . . . . *Cicognara.*

THE DECORATIVE ARTS AND SCULPTURE.

A History of English Furniture . . . . *Percy Macquoid.*
A History of Old English Porcelain . . . *Solon.*

163

Alfred Stevens	*Hugh Stannus.*
Alphabets	*Lewis F. Day.*
Alphabets	*E. Strange.*
Armour in England	*J. Starkie Gardner.*
Art in Chaldea and Assyria, Egypt, Persia, etc. .	*Perrot & Chipiez.*
Art in Needlework	*Day.*
Bases of Design	*Walter Crane.*
Bookbindings in England and France . . .	*W. Y. Fletcher.*
Catalogue of the Spitzer Collection.	
Comment discerner les Styles—	
Architecture, Decoration, Ameublement . .	*Roger Miles.*
XVIII. Century Art in France	,,
Dictionnaire de l'Ameublement	*Havard.*
Dictionnaire du Mobilier Français	*Viollet le Duc.*
Eastern Carpets	*V. J. Robinson.*
Essays on the Art of Pheidias	*C. Waldstein.*
Farbige Decorationen	*Ewald.*
XV. Century Italian Ornament (Painted) . .	*Vacher.*
XV. Century Italian Ornament	*Nicolai.*
French Colour Decoration	*Gélis Didot.*
French Woodcarvings from the National Museums .	*E. Rowe.*
Fresco Decoration	*Gruner.*
Glass Painting	*C. Winston.*
Grammar of Ornament	*Owen Jones.*
Greek and Roman Sculpture	*W. G. Perry.*
Greek Terra Cotta Statuettes	*Marcus B. Huish.*
Greek Vase Painting	*Jane Harrison.*
Hand-book of Greek Archæology	*A. S. Murray.*
Histoire de la Céramique Grecque . . .	*Rayet & Collignon.*
History of English Porcelain	*W. Burton.*
History of Lace	*Mrs. Palliser.*
Illuminated Ornaments from MSS. . . .	*H. Shaw.*
Keramic Art of Japan	*Audsley & Bowes.*
La Broderie	*De Farcy.*
Le Musée de Cluny (Stone and Wood).	
Le Costume Historique	*Racinet.*
Line and Form	*Walter Crane.*
Mediæval Art	*W. J. Lethaby.*
Mediæval Iron Work	*Heftner Alteneck.*
Old English Plate	*W. J. Cripps.*
,, Glasses	*Hartshorne.*
Oriental Carpets from the Austrian Imperial Museum.	
Ornament of Textile Fabrics	*Dupont-Auberville.*
Ornamental Arts of Japan	*Audsley.*
Ornamental Metal Work	*Digby Wyatt.*
Ornamental Textiles	*Fischbach.*
Pictorial Arts of Japan	*Anderson.*
Polychromatic Ornament	*Racinet.*
Pompeian Ornament	*Zahn.*
Stained Glass Windows	*Lewis F. Day.*

The Alhambra	*Owen Jones.*
The Cabinet-maker and Upholsterer's Drawing Book, 1793	*T. Sheraton.*
The Cabinet-maker and Upholsterer's Guide, 1778 .	*A. Hepplewhite.*
The Decorative Work of Robert and James Adam.	
The Gentleman and Cabinet-maker's Director, 1754	*T. Chippendale.*
Trocadéro Museum Sculpture, Illustrations of.	
Tuscan Sculptors	*C. C. Perkins.*

Excellent illustrated articles are in the Portfolio Monographs, *e.g.* :—

1893. English Enamels	*J. Starkie Gardner.*
Greek Terra Cotta Statuettes.	
1898. Greek Bronzes	*A. S. Murray.*
1894. Josiah Wedgwood	*A. H. Church.*
1894. Italian Book Illustrations	*A. W. Pollard.*

Many excellent "Cantor Lectures," by experts, upon the practical application of the Industrial Arts, will be found in the *Society of Arts Journal*, and have been separately published.

The following lectures may be studied with advantage :—

1891. Cloisonné.	1899-1891. Enamels.
1885. Carving and Furniture.	1892. Indian Art.
1891. Decorative Treatment of Natural Foliage.	1897. Material and Design in Pottery.
1898. Decorative Bookbinding.	1904. Maiolica.
1894. Decorative Treatment of Artificial Foliage.	1893. Mosaics.
	1891. Plaster Work.

In the *Builder*, there are the Royal Academy Lectures upon Architecture given by *George Aitchison, R.A.* They include :—

1891. Roman Architecture.	1894. Renascence Architecture.
1892. Saracenic Architecture.	1896. Romanesque Architecture.
1893. Byzantine Architecture.	

In the *Transactions* of the Rochdale Literary Society for 1891 *(Aldine Press)* is a most instructive and well-illustrated article on "The Ornamental Art of Savage People," by *Dr. Hjalmar Stolpe*, translated by Mrs. H. C. March.

The *Transactions* of the Lancashire and Cheshire Antiquarian Society (1891) contain an excellent article upon "The Pagan Christian Overlap in the North," by *H. Colley March, M.D.*

INDEX.

Printed in Dunstable, United Kingdom